Mastering Vocabulary

ANNOTATED INSTRUCTOR'S EDITION

D. J. Henry

Daytona Beach Community College

Susan Pongratz

Thomas Nelson Community College

New York Boston San Francisco
London Toronto Sydney Tokyo Singapore Madrid
Mexico City Munich Paris Cape Town Hong Kong Montreal

Acquisitions Editor: Melanie Craig
Development Editor: Susan Gouijnstook
Marketing Manager: Thomas DeMarco
Senior Supplements Editor: Donna Campion
Media Supplements Editor: Jenna Egan
Production Manager: Ellen MacElree
Project Coordination, Text Design, and Electronic Page Makeup: Nesbitt Graphics, Inc.
Cover Designer/Manager: Wendy Ann Fredericks
Photo Researcher: Chris Pullo
Senior Manufacturing Buyer: Dennis J. Para
Printer and Binder: Quebecor World–Taunton
Cover Printer: Phoenix Color Corps

Library of Congress Cataloging-in-Publication Data on file with the Library of Congress

Please visit us at http://www.ablongman.com/vocabulary

ISBN 0-321-41072-6 (Student Edition)

ISBN 0-321-43449-8 (Instructor's Edition)

1 2 3 4 5 6 7 8 9 10—WCT—09 08 07 06

Contents

Preface vii

UNIT 1
Introduction 1

Study Tips 1

Chapter 1
Vocabulary in Context and Using Word Analysis 5

Chapter 2
Dictionary Skills 36

Unit 1 Review Test 47

UNIT 2
Vocabulary in Health, Nursing, and Science 54

Chapter 3
Vocabulary in Health 54

Chapter 4
Vocabulary in Nursing Fundamentals 62

Chapter 5
Vocabulary in Nursing Issues 70

Chapter 6
Vocabulary in Biology 78

Chapter 7
Vocabulary in Science Issues 86

Unit 2 Review Test 94

UNIT 3
Vocabulary in Social Sciences 99

Chapter 8
Vocabulary in Psychology 99

Chapter 9
Vocabulary in Sociology 108

Chapter 10
Vocabulary in Criminology 116

Chapter 11
Vocabulary in American History 124

Chapter 12
Vocabulary in Current Events 132

Unit 3 Review Test 141

UNIT 4
Vocabulary in Business, Math, and Technology 146

Chapter 13
Vocabulary in Personal Finance 146

Chapter 14
Vocabulary in Business Management 154

Chapter 15
Vocabulary in Statistics 162

Chapter 16
Vocabulary in E-Commerce 171

Chapter 17
Vocabulary in Computer Technology 179

Unit 4 Review Test 187

UNIT 5
Vocabulary in Communications and Humanities 192

Chapter 18
Vocabulary in Interpersonal Communication 192

Chapter 19
Vocabulary in American Literature 200

Chapter 20
Vocabulary in World Literature 208

Chapter 21
Vocabulary in Art History 217

Chapter 22
Vocabulary in Philosophy 224

Unit 5 Review Test 233

APPENDIXES

Appendix A
Word Parts 237

Appendix B
Foreign Words and Phrases 243

Appendix C
Partial Answer Key 244

Preface

Learning new vocabulary requires preparation and practice. Most college students add 2,000 to 3,000 words each year to their reading vocabularies. A knowledge of vocabulary is closely tied to a student's reading comprehension. Since college textbooks contain a great deal of specialized vocabulary, increasing your vocabulary through the study of context clues, word analysis, and dictionary practice will improve your ability to comprehend and communicate.

The chapters in this textbook contain features to provide several encounters with each new word to promote in-depth learning.

Get Ready to Read About

Each chapter begins with an introduction that includes information about a college course and the word parts to help you understand the vocabulary of that subject area.

Vocabulary in Context

We learn most of our vocabulary by watching, listening, and reading, and you will discover in Chapter 1 that recognizing context clues will facilitate your learning. Therefore, unless you are directed to do so, please avoid using a dictionary. However, after you have completed the first exercise, turn to the partial answer key to check your answers.

Synonyms and Antonyms

Each chapter includes an exercise on synonyms and antonyms. Learning a one-word definition (synonym) and learning the opposite meaning (antonym) will provide practice with what the word is and what it is *not.*

Stop and Think

At the end of each chapter, you will find two exercises to help you learn the new words. Whether you are asked to use the words to write a summary or search online for additional information about the word, each activity is designed so that you can work alone or in a study group. Remember, if you encounter the word seven or eight times, you are more likely to remember its definition and the correct way to use it.

The Teaching and Learning Package

Longman is pleased to offer a variety of support materials to help make teaching vocabulary easier on teachers and to help students excel in their coursework. Contact your local Longman sales representative for more information on pricing and how to create a package.

An **Annotated Instructor's Edition (0-321-43449-8)** is available to Instructors. The Annotated Instructor's Edition is an exact replica of the student edition with the answers included.

Vocabulary Skills Study Card (Student/ 0-321-31802-1)
Colorful, affordable, and packed with useful information, Longman's Vocabulary Study Card is a concise, 8-page reference guide to developing key vocabulary skills, such as learning to recognize context clues, reading a dictionary entry, and recognizing key root words, suffixes, and prefixes. Laminated for durability, students can keep this Study Card for years to come and pull it out whenever they need a quick review.

Oxford American College Dictionary (Student / 0-399-14415-3)
A hard cover reference with more than 175,000 entries.

The New American Webster Handy College Dictionary (Student / 0-451-18166-2)
A paperback reference text with more than 100,000 entries.

Multimedia Offerings

Interested in incorporating online materials into your course? Longman is happy to help. Our regional technology specialists provide training on all of our multimedia offerings.

MyReadingLab (www.myreadinglab.com)
This exciting new website houses all the media tools any developmental English student will need to improve their reading and study skills, and all in one easy-to-use place.

Other Books in This Series

Book 1: Developing Vocabulary (0-321-41070-X)
Book 2: Effective Vocabulary (0-321-41071-8)

Acknowledgments

We are indebted to the many reviewers for their invaluable contributions. We would especially like to thank the following reviewers for their suggestions and guidance: Stephen Drinane, SUNY Rockland Community College; Flo J Hill, Albany State University; Evelyn Koperwas, Broward Community College; Carrie H. Pyhrr, Austin Community College; Florinda Rodriguez, South Texas College; and Wendy Wish, Valencia Community College.

Many people have helped make this project a gratifying journey. My campus colleague and good friend Mary Dubbé emboldened me to persevere. I thank her for balance, direction, and encouragement. My best virtual friend Janet Elder provided inspiration and levity in some of the most uncanny and well-timed communications. The connection is inexplicably delightful. For the artwork and photographs, I thank Molly Gamble-Walker, George Pongratz, and Elizabeth Pongratz. May their muses continue to provide. The muses of the staff and fellows of the Eastern Virginia Writing Project, Summer Institute 2006 helped me fill the well, particularly Andrew Sargent, who taught me to "eat poetry" and Nicole Throckmorton, who provided tutelage as the designated hitter. Likewise, I am grateful for the patience, suggestions, and gracious attention from my editor Susan Gouijnstook, who continues to give me courage in the quietest of ways. Thanks also to Melanie Craig, acquisitions editor, Ellen MacElree, senior production editor, and Rona Tucillo, visual research manager. Finally, I gratefully acknowledge the talented and incomparable Kathy Smith for scrutinizing, sifting, raking, editing, proofing, fixing, polishing, and encouraging me during the writing of all three books.

—Susan Pongratz

It is such a thrill to partner with Susan Pongratz, a gifted teacher and writer, to provide this comprehensive vocabulary program. It is so gratifying to work with a kindred spirit who shares a deep devotion to students and clear vision for their academic success. In talent, creativity, and dedication, none can compare to Susan Pongratz, and I thank her for giving so much of herself. I would also like to thank Susan Gouijnstook, Developmental Editor, and Melanie Craig, Acquisitions Editor, for their faith in our work. Finally, I would like to thank all of you who allow us to partner with you in your classroom instruction. It is an honor to be a part of your life's work!

—D. J. Henry

UNIT 1 Introduction

STUDY Tips

Throughout this book, you will be asked to practice using and working with new words. By creating study cards, you will enhance your in-depth knowledge of the words. Study the models to determine new ways of learning vocabulary.

Frayer Model

To complete a modified Frayer Model, follow these steps.
Write the word in the center of the card.

1. Write definition/synonyms (one-word definitions) of the word.
2. Write characteristics or other forms of the word.
3. Write the antonyms.
4. Write a non-example (people, things, descriptions of what the word is not).

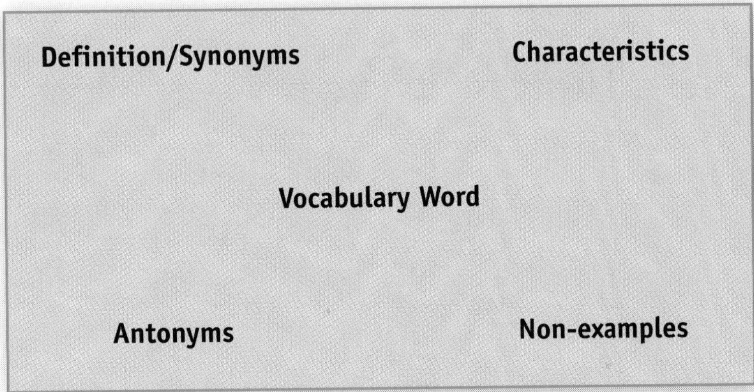

Example 1

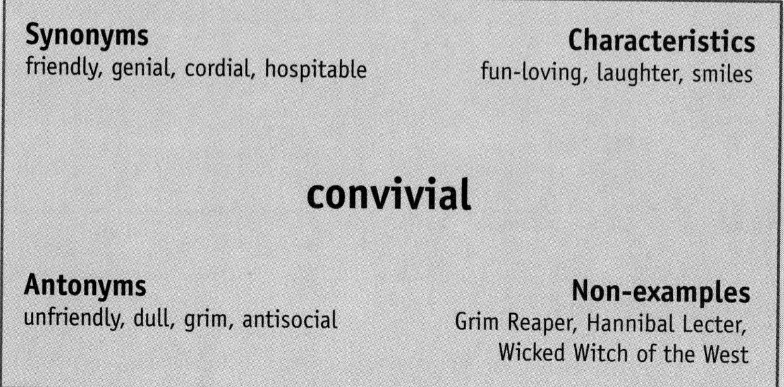
Synonyms
friendly, genial, cordial, hospitable
Characteristics
fun-loving, laughter, smiles
convivial
Antonyms
unfriendly, dull, grim, antisocial
Non-examples
Grim Reaper, Hannibal Lecter,
Wicked Witch of the West

Example 2

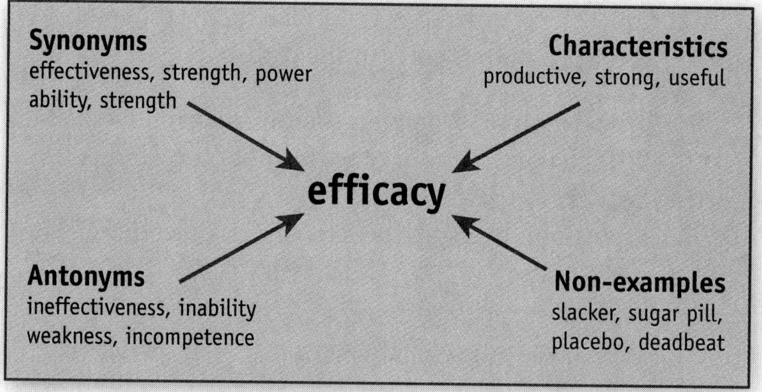
Synonyms
effectiveness, strength, power
ability, strength
Characteristics
productive, strong, useful
efficacy
Antonyms
ineffectiveness, inability
weakness, incompetence
Non-examples
slacker, sugar pill,
placebo, deadbeat

Visual Vocabulary Cards

Another way to learn new vocabulary words is to create cards with sketches or pictures to help you visualize the word and the definition. For example, to learn the word *lethargic,* which means *exhausted,* imagine a tired dog resting on a wall, too tired to play. The image will help you connect the word and its meaning.

Example

Molly Gamble-Walker

Pyramid Summary

1. Write the vocabulary word.
2. List three synonyms (one-word definitions).
3. List the word parts and definitions (if available).
4. List antonyms (opposites) of the word.
5. Write a sentence using the word.

brouhaha

uproar, noise, commotion

French cry used in medieval theater; loud, confusing noise

peace, serenity, silence, tranquility, calm, stillness, quiet, agreement

No one understood the purpose of the brouhaha, but it caused everyone to take notice.

KIM

Divide the index card into three columns.

1. Write the vocabulary word in column 1.
2. Write any information you have about the word, such as the definition, synonyms, antonyms, and a sentence in column 2.
3. Create a drawing that represents the word in column 3.

Key Word	Information	Mental Image
Write the vocabulary word.	Write the definition, synonym, antonym, sentence.	Draw a picture.

Example

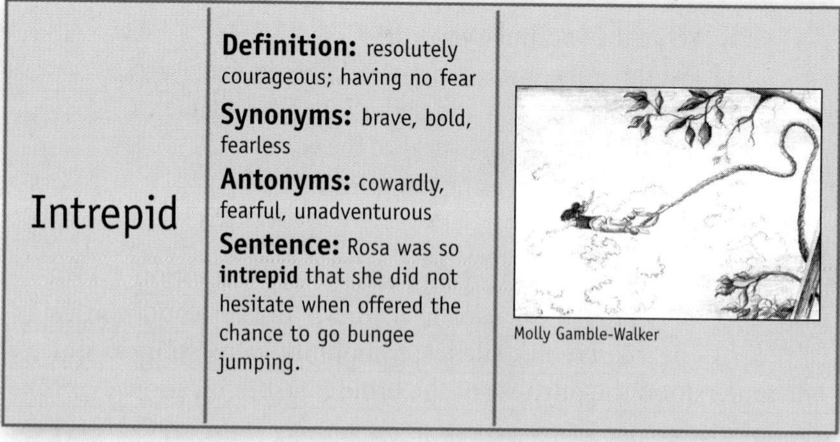

Intrepid	**Definition:** resolutely courageous; having no fear **Synonyms:** brave, bold, fearless **Antonyms:** cowardly, fearful, unadventurous **Sentence:** Rosa was so **intrepid** that she did not hesitate when offered the chance to go bungee jumping.	Molly Gamble-Walker

CHAPTER

1

Vocabulary in Context and Using Word Analysis

Get Ready to Read About Context Clues and Word Analysis

A good vocabulary is one of the elements of academic success. Adding to your personal inventory of words is an ongoing process that requires knowledge of context clues and word parts. As you read through this chapter, consider your prior knowledge about the following words:

Vocabulary—the words used or understood by a person
Context clue—information that surrounds a new word and is used to understand its meaning
Synonym—a word that has the same or nearly the same meaning as another word
Antonym—a word that has the opposite meaning of another word
Prefix—a group of letters with a specific meaning that is added to the beginning of a word to form a new word
Root—the foundation of a word
Suffix—a group of letters with a specific meaning that is added to the end of a word to form a new meaning (Suffixes may also change the part of speech of a word.)

My parents came to New York from Russia when I was three. They knew the Cyrillic and Hebrew alphabets, but not the Roman, so I learned to read under difficulties. I memorized a jump-rope rhyme with the letters of the alphabet, but I thought they were just nonsense syllables. When I realized it was the alphabet, I got older kids to write the letters down for me, and I would practice writing them.—Isaac Asimov

Source: "Seven Headliners Tell What It Took to Turn Them into Readers," *American School Board Journal,* August, 1985, the National School Board Association. Bruce Publishing Co., 1985.

Words Are Building Blocks

Vocabulary is all the words used or understood by a person.

Isaac Asimov eventually became a well-known author of more than 300 books. You will notice that learning new words is like creating a structure. You begin with a foundation on which you continue to build as a lifelong learner.

How many words do you have in your vocabulary? At the age of 4, you only knew about 5,600 words. By the age of 10, you had increased that number to about 34,000. If you are like most people, by the time you are 18 years old, you know about 60,000 words. In one college year, however, you will double that to 120,000. During your entire college studies, you will most likely learn an additional 20,000 words. Each subject you study will have its own set of words. There are several ways to study vocabulary.

Source: //www.ucc.vt.edu/stdysk/vocabula.html retrieved 11/01/2005 and Henry, D.J., *The Effective Reader.*

Vocabulary in Context

Define the following words. (Answers will vary.)

1. conch ______________________________.

2. fluking ______________________________.

3. scuttered ______________________________.

4. strident ______________________________.

5. wubber ______________________________.

Now read the selection below.

"His ordinary voice sounded like a whisper after the harsh note of the **conch.** He laid the conch against his lips, took a deep breath and blew once more. The note boomed again: and then at his firmer pressure, the note, **fluking** up an octave, became a **strident** blare more penetrating than before. Piggy was shouting something, his face pleased, his glasses flashing. The birds cried, small animals **scuttered.** Ralph's breath failed; the note dropped the octave, became a low **wubber,** was a rush of air."

—Golding, William, *Lord of the Flies*, Penguin Putnam Inc., 1954. p. 16.

Select the best definition for each word.

1. Walking along the shoreline after the storm, we discovered an impressive pink and cameo-colored **conch,** but it was no longer home to any marine animal.

__d__ **Conch** means

a. ancient coin.
b. smooth stone.
c. sea glass.
d. shell for a mollusk.

2. Driving around the area, we were **fluking** for a chance bargain, and discovered a "For Sale By Owner" sign on a charming cottage.

__a__ **Fluking** means

a. getting something by luck.
b. struggling to get rid of something.
c. losing without noticing.
d. listening for animal sounds.

3. The campus squirrels are fearless, looking for food, **scuttering** near students eating their lunch on the lawn.

__b__ **Scutter** means

a. sleep.
b. move quickly.
c. hide.
d. polish.

4. Following their conversation in the huddle before the game, all of the players gave a **strident** *Whoop!* and then ran to the sidelines.

__c__ **Strident** means

a. quiet.
b. serious.
c. loud.
d. polite.

5. His disagreement with the director was only a **wubber**, a soft sigh, in comparison to the other co-workers' loud praise.

__a__ **Wubber** means

a. whisper.
b. reasonable concern.
c. joke.
d. note of sympathy.

Answers: 1. d 2. a 3. b 4. c 5. a

The preceding example from the novel *Lord of the Flies,* written in 1954 by Englishman William Golding, gives a sample of rich vocabulary that includes words you may know, words known as *colloquialisms* (words from a local or regional dialect), and technical words from a specific academic area such as music. Although the book is an exciting adventure tale about boys stranded on an uncharted island after a plane crash, the language can be challenging. A strong vocabulary is critical for comprehension, and knowing how to use context clues is also an important way to understand the meaning of new words.

Successful college students know how to interact with new words in a number of ways. One way is to use context clues. The meaning of a word is shaped by its context. The word *context* means "surroundings." Effective readers use context clues to learn new words.

A **context clue** is the information that surrounds a new word, used to understand its meaning.

The four most common types of context clues are:

- Synonyms
- Antonyms
- General context
- Examples

Notice that when you put together the first letter of each context clue, it spells the word **SAGE.** The word *sage* means "wise." Using context clues is a wise—a **SAGE**—reading strategy, and this mnemonic device, or memory trick, will help you recall the kinds of context clues writers use.

Synonyms

A **synonym** is a word that has the same or nearly the same meaning as another word. You can remember this because the prefix *syn-* means *same* and the root *nym* means *name*. For example, the words *amorphous* and *vague* are synonyms since they both have similar meanings. Many times, an author will place a synonym near a new or difficult word as a context clue to the word's meaning. Usually, a synonym is set off with a pair of commas, a pair of dashes, or within a pair of parentheses.

Synonym Signal Words				
also known as	*by this we mean*	*in other words*	*or*	*that is*

VISUAL VOCABULARY

Our history professor is **devoid** of, or completely without, a sense of humor, even when we try to make a humorous comment about the subject.

Devoid means

b ______

a. full.
b. lacking.
c. serious.
d. sad.

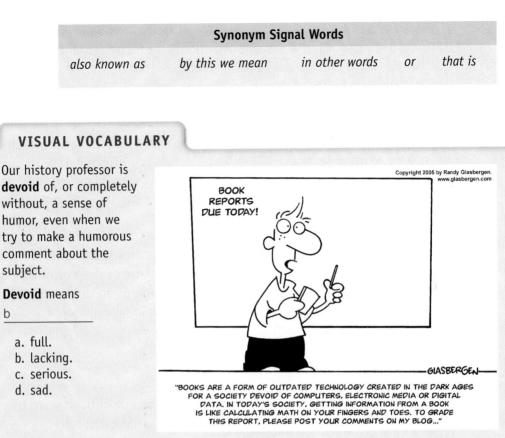

Copyright 2005 by Randy Glasbergen.
www.glasbergen.com
BOOK REPORTS DUE TODAY!
GLASBERGEN
"BOOKS ARE A FORM OF OUTDATED TECHNOLOGY CREATED IN THE DARK AGES FOR A SOCIETY DEVOID OF COMPUTERS, ELECTRONIC MEDIA OR DIGITAL DATA. IN TODAY'S SOCIETY, GETTING INFORMATION FROM A BOOK IS LIKE CALCULATING MATH ON YOUR FINGERS AND TOES. TO GRADE THIS REPORT, PLEASE POST YOUR COMMENTS ON MY BLOG..."

Antonyms

An **antonym** is a word that has the opposite meaning of another word. For example, *collegial* (mutually respectful) and *hostile* (unfriendly) are antonyms. Antonyms help you see the shade of a word's meaning by showing you what the original word is *not.* The following contrast words often act as signals that an antonym is being used.

Antonym Signal Words		
although	however	on the other hand
but	in contrast	unlike
conversely	instead	whereas
despite	nevertheless	yet
even though	not	

Sometimes antonyms can be found next to the new word. In those cases, commas, dashes, or parentheses set them off. At other times, antonyms are placed in other parts of the sentence to emphasize the contrast between the ideas.

General Context

Often you will find that the author has not provided either a synonym clue or an antonym clue. In that case, you will have to rely on the general context of the passage to figure out the meaning of the unfamiliar word. This requires you to read the entire sentence, or to read ahead for the next few sentences, for information that will help you understand the new word.

Information about the word can be included in the passage in several ways. Sometimes a definition of the word may be presented. Vivid word pictures or descriptions of a situation can provide a sense of the word's meaning. Sometimes you may need to figure out the meaning of an unknown word by using logic and reasoning skills based on your personal experience and background knowledge.

Examples

Many times an author will show the meaning of a new or difficult word by providing an example. Signal words indicate that an example is coming.

Example Signal Words			
consists of	*for instance*	*like*	*to illustrate*
for example	*including*	*such as*	

Colons and dashes can also indicate examples.

In addition to using context clues for vocabulary improvement, a master reader will study visual images and captions provided in textbooks. Likewise, a good reader will study graphs, charts, photographs, and cartoons.*

SAGE		
Context Clue	**Example**	**Definition**
Synonym	The campaign posters in their yard indicate the Walkers are **ostensibly,** or apparently, planning to vote for a different candidate from last time.	*Ostensibly* means *apparently* or *evidently*.
Antonym	The constant arguing only **attenuates** the committee rather than helping it grow stronger.	*Attenuate* means *weaken*.
General Context	The new computer program has been improved with many features that make it much more **robust** than the earlier version.	*Robust* means *powerfully built*.
Example	Historic examples of **imperialism** include the British and French government policies in Africa and the Americas.	*Imperialism* is the policy of extending your rule over foreign countries.

**Source:* D. J. Henry, *The Master Reader.*

VISUAL VOCABULARY

Study the cartoon and then choose the best definition of the word in **bold** print.

It's difficult to find a **rural** area that is not being overdeveloped, but traveling to the countryside often provides a chance for quiet from the busy world of the city.

Rural means a________

a. country. c. crowded.
b. city. d. noisy.

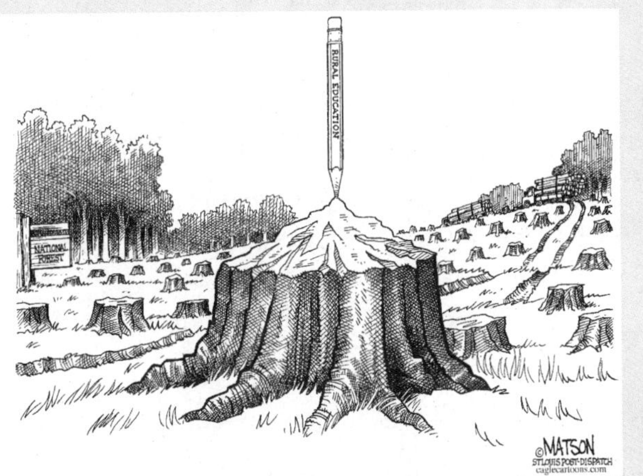

© R. J. Matson/The St. Louis Dispatch, Cagle Cartoons

EXERCISE 1 Synonym Clues

A. Select the letter of the best definition for the word in **bold** print.

1. The speaker's **egregious** grammatical error was so distracting that many in the audience missed a good message because of the subject–verb agreement mistake.

__b__ **Egregious** means

a. hardly noticeable. c. boring.
b. remarkably bad. d. simple

2. The most **lamentable,** or regrettable, episode of his life was flirting with the French woman during his study abroad experience, which resulted in losing his girlfriend who had faithfully waited for him back at school.

__c__ **Lamentable** means

a. famous. c. regrettable.
b. quiet. d. praiseworthy.

3. She was rarely taken seriously because of her **errant** flights of unusual and adventurous ideas.

__d__ **Errant** means

a. dull. b. ordinary. c. planned. d. wandering.

4. Emily tried to coax the **feral** cats in her neighborhood to eat the food she set out for them, but she knew the wild animals were often fearful around people.

__a__ **Feral** means

a. untamed. b. tame. c. calm. d. friendly.

5. Negotiations did not **appease** the unfriendly country, and any additional attempts to satisfy that country caused conflict at home.

__a__ **Appease** means

a. calm. b. anger. c. promise. d. enjoy.

B. Fill in the blank with the meaning of the word in **bold** print.

6. Janet took one look at her roommate's new outfit and made a **caustic**—that is, sarcastic—comment about her new look.

Caustic means __sarcastic__.

7. In an effort to **quell** the outrage over the recent news of a mishandling of funds, the administration offered to start sharing information with honesty, which helped control public anger.

Quell means control ______________.

8. **Ursprache,** or parent language, was the last word in a National Spelling Bee Challenge.

Ursprache means parent language ______________.

9. Because the pitcher had been **sniping** at his teammate for several days, the coach finally benched him until he had a chance to consider how his criticizing was hurting team spirit.

Snipe means criticize ______________.

10. "We found an excellent carpenter who can copy anything," explained Sandy, "because all we did was show him a photograph of a porch we liked and he was able to **replicate** it."

Replicate means copy ______________.

EXERCISE 2 Antonym Clues

A. Select the letter of the best definition for the word in **bold** print.

1. Sterling is so sensitive and polite, unlike his roommate, who is an obvious **boor.**

c **Boor** means
a. ambitious person.
b. quiet and polite person.
c. insensitive and rude person.
d. interesting person.

2. Although she is fun-loving and full of humor, Sara tried to present a **staid** appearance when she was a bridesmaid for her best friend.

b **Staid** means
a. adventurous and impulsive.
b. serious and calm.
c. wild and crazy.
d. loud and impolite.

3. A **blatant** disregard for the rules seems to be more upsetting to people than one that is done deliberately and secretly, showing an effort to avoid getting caught.

a **Blatant** means
a. obvious. b. secret. c. unappreciative. d. quiet.

4. Because of the potential damage oxygen poses to most material, ancient documents must be stored in **hermetic** cases rather than in ones that are not sealed.

__d__ **Hermetic** means
a. locked.
b. well-lit.
c. expensive.
d. airtight.

5. "To be a leader," Lindsay's father advised, "you must be someone who **ameliorates** a situation instead of making it worse."

__a__ **Ameliorate** means
a. improve.
b. destroy.
c. ignore.
d. increase.

B. Fill in the blank with the meaning of the word in **bold** print.

6. Even under great stress, James exhibits **equanimity;** however, it is his roommate who flies off the handle and loses his patience when things get difficult.

Equanimity means evenness of mind.

7. A **sagacious** friend is honest and true—someone who will give good advice, whereas a foolish friend will often lead you down the wrong path.

Sagacious means wise.

8. In spite of the initial criticism that she would prove to be a weak and insignificant candidate, the congressional hopeful proved to be a **formidable** fundraiser.

Formidable means impressive and effective.

9. Instead of simply being **wary** of the things that they don't know about or understand, college students learn to be more trusting and less cautious though education.

Wary means cautious.

10. Zach's statistics professor **mesmerized** the class during each lecture, making relevant connections to real life; on the other hand, his history instructor was always boring.

Mesmerize means fascinate.

EXERCISE 3 General Context Clues

A. Select the letter of the best definition for the word in **bold** print.

1. Following the death of his father, the young golfer was **inconsolable** because he had lost his caddy, his mentor, and his best friend.

__c__ **Inconsolable** means
a. uplifted.
b. triumphant.
c. grief-stricken.
d. light-hearted.

2. As a result of the **debacle** of allowing his ship to drift into the path of an oncoming vessel, the captain was relieved of his command and reassigned to a desk job.

__a__ **Debacle** means
a. disaster.
b. good fortune.
c. spirit.
d. poverty.

3. The glassblower confessed that the life of an artist can be a lonely one, so he forces himself to socialize with friends to avoid being a **recluse.**

__b__ **Recluse** means
a. celebrity. b. loner. c. executive. d. superstar.

4. The **spurious** comments about the popular student were part of a gossip campaign from a group of hateful students known for spreading lies.

__a__ **Spurious** means
a. false.
b. complimentary.
c. instructive
d. genuine.

5. The speaker's **exhortation** to support his cause was so passionate and convincing that we all felt inclined to join in.

__c__ **Exhortation** means
a. hilarious speech.
b. disappointing speech.
c. persuasive speech.
d. boring speech.

B. Fill in the blank with the meaning of the word in **bold** print.

6. The lawyer reminded the jury that because the defendant's crime was so **heinous,** he should be found guilty, and they should recommend the most severe punishment.

Heinous means monstrous or shocking.

7. Following the six weeks of having his arm in a cast, Raul was scheduled for physical therapy because muscles can **atrophy** if they are not exercised for an extended period of time.

Atrophy means weaken or deteriorate.

8. Because Charlie has a **predilection** toward disorganization, he has to take time out every six weeks to rearrange and clean his shop.

Predilection means natural tendency.

9. For many who try out for *American Idol*, theirs is a **fugacious** ambition that lasts only a short time.

Fugacious means passing quickly away.

10. Early each morning, Mr. Cortina arranges his produce in the front of his **bodega.**

Bodega means small grocery store.

EXERCISE 4 Example Clues

A. Select the letter of the best definition for the word in **bold** print.

1. When one spouse makes a **unilateral** decision without consulting his or her partner about something major such as the purchase of a vehicle or a home, then this may indicate a breakdown in communication.

d **Unilateral** means
a. dependent. b. careless. c. joint. d. one-sided.

2. **Obelisks** such as the Washington Monument, the Bunker Hill Monument, and Chipley Monument are similar to the architecture ancient Egyptians used to flank the entrances of some of their temples.

c **Obelisk** means
a. pyramid.
b. flat room surrounded by steps.
c. tall, thin, four-sided tapered monument.
d. circular rotunda covering a meeting area.

3. Famous **aphorisms** such as Benjamin Franklin's "A penny saved is twopence clear" and "Fish and visitors stink in three days" have been quoted and printed many times.

__a__ **Aphorism** means
a. saying. b. book. c. photograph. d. play.

4. Some of the most **infamous** events in United States history, including Pearl Harbor, the Wounded Knee Massacre, the battle of Bull Run, and the internment of Japanese Americans during World War II include stories that not all history students have been allowed to study.

__b__ **Infamous** means
a. successful. c. happy.
b. having a bad reputation. d. patriotic.

5. There are three categories of **miscreants** that oppose the X-men heroes and heroines: Acolytes members, the Brotherhood of Evil mutants, and the Hellions.

__c__ **Miscreant** means
a. innocent person. c. evil-doer.
b. leader. d. hero.

B. Fill in the blank with the meaning of the word in **bold** print.

6. Twentieth century **despots** who ruled with absolute power include Mussolini, Hitler, and Stalin.

Despot means dictator.

7. Acts of **obeisance** such as a curtsy, a bow, or a gracious nod can be misinterpreted as signs of weakness, when they actually indicate good manners.

Obeisance means gesture or attitude of respect.

8. Upon meeting Richard, we first thought he was very clever because he only spoke using famous movie lines such as, "You had me at *hello*" or "Looks like it's open season on mutants again" or "It's okay, I wouldn't remember me either"; however, this **vapid** style of communication soon became tiresome.

Vapid means dull, boring, uninteresting.

9. A **hierarchy** exists in all aspects of a culture, including the ranking order in a college administration, a football team, an executive board room, the military, and even religious orders.

Hierarchy means chain of command.

10. College athletics is becoming a more **sordid** enterprise as we hear about athletes who are given special treatment or valuable gifts and are also able to avoid conviction for unlawful acts.

Sordid means disgusting; unpleasant.

EXERCISE 5 Vocabulary in Context

A. Select the letter of the best definition for the word in **bold** print.

1. His charming smile **belies** his true nature, which is deceptive and cruel.

b **Belie** means

a. reveal. c. imagine.
b. disguise. d. examine.

2. The child's **churlish** nature embarrassed his parents, who were always courteous and well-mannered.

c **Churlish** means

a. pleasant. c. rude.
b. impatient. d. courteous.

3. Many classic novels such as *Ulysses* by James Joyce and *Cry, the Beloved Country* by Alan Paton have an **epiphany** as a theme in which the main character experiences a sudden revelation of a universal truth.

a **Epiphany** means

a. revelation. c. arrangement of heroes.
b. gradual disappointment. d. example of mistaken identity.

4. When the **hegemony** in a country becomes too oppressive, the domination can lead to a major uprising and eventual overthrowing of those in authority.

c **Hegemony** means

a. obedience. c. leadership.
b. ease. d. grace.

5. Winston Churchill said, "The truth is **incontrovertible;** malice may attack it, ignorance may deride it; but in the end, there it is."

d **Incontrovertible** means

a. unworthy. c. unimportant.
b. suspicious. d. undeniable.

B. Fill in the blank with the meaning of the word in **bold** print.

6. Each evening during dinner, Diane's father would present scenarios of things that might happen in order to **inculcate** ideas about good work ethics and appropriate behavior.

Inculcate means instill.

7. At the beginning of his freshman year, Andrew decided to study word origins to increase the words in his personal **lexicon** and thus improve his communication skills.

Lexicon means vocabulary.

8. Before deciding on a marketing strategy, the team studied several successful **paradigms** of similar companies and then selected one example everyone thought would succeed.

Paradigm means example or model.

9. While writing our persuasive paper, we learned that the next to the last paragraph is the most important, and then in the last paragraph we should **recapitulate,** or summarize, our ideas.

Recapitulate means summarize or sum up.

10. The student teachers were informed about the requirements for obtaining a teaching certificate as well as the names of other states with which an agreement of **reciprocity** existed so they could determine all areas in which a mutual agreement of credentials occurred.

Reciprocity means mutual agreement.

Word Analysis

Just as ideas are made up of words, words are also made up of smaller parts. Learning word parts can help you learn vocabulary more easily and quickly. In addition, knowing the meaning of the parts of words helps you understand the meaning of a new word when you first encounter it. It can also help you memorize the definition. Finally, learning word parts can help you improve your spelling ability when you are writing. In fact, the word *misspell* is a combination of the prefix *mis-*, which means *wrong*, and the root *spell*. Many words are divided into the following three parts: roots, prefixes, and suffixes.

Study the chart below to see the role word parts play in vocabulary development by considering the parts of the word *symbiotic.*

Root	Foundation of the word	*bio*	life
Prefix	Found at the beginning of a word	*sym-*	same
Suffix	Found at the end of a word	*-ic*	characteristic of

VISUAL VOCABULARY

Study the cartoon to determine the definition.
The word *symbiotic* means c.

a. enemy.
b. relationship of zoo animals.
c. relationship of mutual benefit.
d. relationship of mammals.

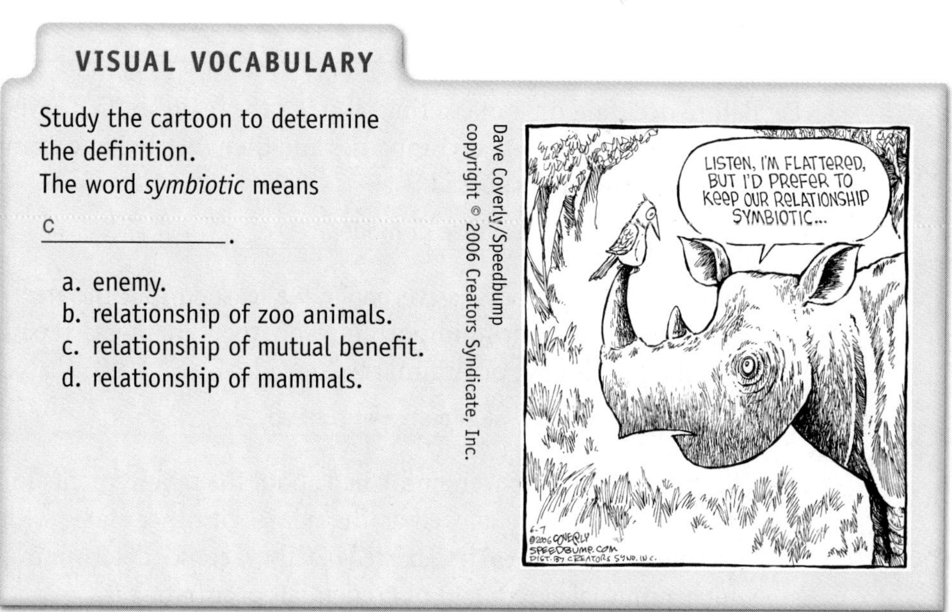

Dave Coverly/Speedbump copyright © 2006 Creators Syndicate, Inc.

Root Words

The roots of words form the foundation. Many of our root words come from Latin and Greek words. Learning to recognize the roots of words will help you understand the meanings of many new words.

EXAMPLE Write meanings of the following words:

abiogenesis, amphibious, antibiotic, autobiography, biochemistry, biocidal, biodegradable, biogenesis, biography, biology, biometry, biopsy, biota, symbiotic

abiogenesis (development of life from nonliving things), *amphibious* (able to live in water and on land), *antibiotic* (antibacterial material produced by living organisms), *autobiog-*

raphy (story of someone's life written by that person), *biochemistry* (science that deals with the chemical processes of living things), *biocidal* (causing the death of life), *biodegradable* (capable of decomposing), *biography* (story of a person's life by another person), *biology* (study of living organisms), *biometry* (measuring of the probable duration of a person's life), *biopsy* (diagnosis from living tissue), *biota* (living plants and animals in a region), *symbiotic* (characterized by the existence of two different organisms mutually dependent on each other)

EXPLANATION Each of the words has the root *bio,* which comes from the Latin word that means *life*. By adding a prefix, another root, or a suffix to that foundation, new words are formed.

EXERCISE 1 Root Words

Study the following words and their definitions to determine the meaning of each root:

1. proclaim: to announce officially
clamor: a loud, sustained noise
claimant: person who demands something rightfully due

___b___ *Clam, claim* mean
a. make legal.
b. cry out.
c. quiet.
d. satisfy.

2. ecosystem: interrelated community of plants, animals, and bacteria
economy: management of income in the environment
ecology: branch of biology that deals with living things and their habitat

___c___ *Eco* means
a. science.
b. money.
c. environment.
d. finance.

3. facilitate: make easier
facetious: giving a witty impression
facile: done easily

___b___ *Fac* means
a. destroy. b. make, do. c. laugh. d. prove false.

4. inference: conclusion
transfer: move across
interfere: come in between for some purpose

__c__ *Fere* means
a. build. b. design. c. carry. d. plant.

5. dissect: separate into sections
intersect: cut across
sector: part of a circle bounded by two radii and the arc between them

__c__ *Sect* means
a. preach. b. straighten. c. cut. d. encircle.

6. antipathy: a feeling of dislike
apathy: lacking feeling
empathy: deep understanding of another's feelings

__a__ *Path, pathy* mean
a. feeling. b. sorrow. c. dislike. d. sadness.

7. philanthropist: one who loves humanity
philharmonic: pertaining to an organization of the those who love music
philanderer: an unfaithful man

__b__ *Phil* means
a. beginning. b. love. c. humanity. d. music.

8. Anglophobia: dislike of England or the English
monophobia: fear of being alone
agoraphobia: fear of open spaces

__b__ *Phobia* means
a. thanks. b. fear. c. crowd. d. alone.

9. tripod: three-footed stool
podiatrist: foot doctor
podium: raised platform; low wall that serves as a foundation

__b__ *Pod* means
a. stool. b. foot. c. wall. d. doctor.

10. geocentric: having the earth as the center
geomorphic: pertaining to the shape of the earth
geophysics: sciences studying the forces that affect the earth

__d__ *Geo* means
a. beauty. b. change. c. force. d. earth.

EXERCISE 2 Root Words

Study the chart below and insert a second example of a word that contains each root. (Answers will vary.)

Root Words Guide

Root	Example	Example
autre, alter	alteration	________
bio	biology	________
capere/capt	caption	________
celer	accelerate	________
clam/claim/clamere	exclaim	________
clima	climate	________
clude/clus	include	________
commodare	accommodate	________
derm	hypodermic	________
dext	dexterity	________
eco	ecosystem	________
err	errant	________
fac	facade	________
fer	transfer	________
ferv	fervor	________
gamos	monogamous	________
genne	genetic	________
graph	photography	________
icon	iconoclast	________
insula	insulate	________
junct	conjunction	________
lith	monolith	________
logos	dialog	________
nomous	autonomous	________
oper	operate	________
pend	independent	________
pharyngy	pharyngitis	________

Root	Example	Example
pond	ponderous	________
port	portable	________
press	expressive	________
psych	psychology	________
sect	dissect	________
sembl	resemblance	________
simul	simulate	________
spect	inspection	________
sphere	biosphere	________
stance	instance	________
stimulus	stimulation	________
struct	construction	________
sumere	consumption	________
therm	thermal	________
tract	extract	________
troph	trophic	________
vapor	vaporize	________

Prefixes

A prefix appears at the beginning of a word and changes the meaning of a word. In fact, *pre-* means *before.* For instance, consider the word *moral,* which means *ethical* and *honest.* If you add the prefix *a-*, however, you negate the word, or change its meaning to a negative word, *amoral,* which means *unprincipled* and *dishonorable.* If you arrange the prefixes into categories, it is easier to remember them. Look at the examples below.

Negative	Placement	Numbers	Time
a- (not)	*ab-* (away)	*uni-* (one)	*ante-* (before)
un- (not)	*circum-* (around)	*bi-* (two)	*pre-* (before)
il- (not)	*hypo-* (under, below)	*tri-* (three)	*post-* (after)
anti- (against)	*sub-* (under, below)	*cent-* (hundred)	*re-* (again)
mis- (wrong)	*peri-* (around)	*multi-* (many)	*retro-* (back)
mal- (bad)	*pro-* (for, forward)	*poly-* (many)	*inter-* (during)

EXAMPLE Following a winter hiking **mishap** in the snow-covered mountains in which Jan suffered **hypothermia** from his overexposure to the elements, doctors consulted in a **post-surgery** meeting to discuss their **prognosis** before talking with him and his family.

Mishap means disaster.
Hypothermia means below normal body temperature.
Post-surgery means after surgery.
Prognosis means prediction or forecast of the chance of recovery or outcome.

EXPLANATION The prefix *mis-* means *wrong* or *bad,* so a *mishap* is related to a disaster or tragedy. The prefix *hypo-* means *below* and the root *therm* means *heat,* so his body temperature in the cold weather dropped dangerously below normal. Since the prefix *post-* means *after,* the doctors are discussing their patient's status after the surgery has occurred. And since the prefix *pro-* means forward and the root *gnosis* means *to know,* they are considering their prediction based on information they know to determine the patient's possible chances for recovery.

Note: You will notice that sometimes, several prefixes have the same meaning. For example, *sub-* and *hypo-* both mean *under* or *below.* Likewise, *circum-* and *peri-* mean *around.* Because many of the word parts are derived from Latin and Greek words, you will discover several with the same meaning as well as some with multiple meanings. The prefix *a-*, for example, can mean *not* or *without* as in *atypical* (unusual) or *apolitical* (without interest in politics), or *on* as in *aboard* or *ashore,* or *away from* as in *awry* (off-course) or *avert* (avoid). Other examples include *im-* , which means *not* in the word *imperfect,* but in the word *impassioned,* that same prefix increases the value so the word means *very passionate* or *fervent.* Likewise, although *in-* means *not,* the word *invaluable* means *irreplaceable.* Something invaluable is so precious that its value cannot be measured. As you can see, it is important to recognize multiple meanings in word parts.

EXERCISE 1 Prefixes

Study the following words and their definitions to determine the definition of each prefix.

1. transient: passing quickly
transpose: shift or interchange
transmute: change from one form to another

a *Trans-* means
a. across; change. b. again. c. around. d. close; near.

2. ambivalent: having mixed feelings
ambiguous: having more than one meaning
ambient: surrounding on all sides

__c__ *Ambi-* means
a. beginning. b. mind. c. both. d. surface.

3. misandry: hatred of men
misspell: incorrect spelling
misogynist: a person who hates women

__b__ *Mis-* means
a. in a backward way.
b. wrong; bad; hate.
c. having to do with humans.
d. having to do with words.

4. circumference: distance around
circumvent: avoid; getting around a problem
circumnavigate: travel completely around

__c__ *Circum-* means
a. under. b. before. c. around. d. above.

5. neophyte: beginner
neoanthropic: pertaining to new forms of humanity
neonatal: newly born

__a__ *Neo-* means
a. new. b. first. c. perfect. d. stone.

6. polyarchy: government by many persons
polyglot: someone who speaks many languages
polymorphism: occurrence of different forms, stages, or types of individuals or organisms

__d__ *Poly-* means
a. change; across.
b. power.
c. one.
d. many.

7. eugenics: study of using selective breeding to control the growth of members of a particular group
eulogize: praise in speaking or writing
euphony: agreeable, pleasant sound

__c__ *Eu-* means
a. alone.
b. separate.
c. good; well; true.
d. many.

8. endocrine: secreting internally
endoskeleton: internal supporting skeleton
endocardium: thin membrane lining the interior of the heart

__a__ *Endo-* means

a. inside. b. outside. c. under. d. around.

9. concurrent: happening at the same time
congenial: friendly with others
congruent: in agreement

__d__ *Con-* means

a. one. b. alone. c. front. d. with; together.

10. disaster: sudden calamity
dispassionate: without emotion or bias
disperse: scatter to all parts of an area

__a__ *Dis-* means

a. apart; not. c. simple.
b. connected. d. near.

EXERCISE 2 Prefixes

Study the chart below and insert a second example of a word that contains each prefix. (Answers will vary.)

Prefixes Guide

Prefix	Example	Example
a-	atypical	________
ac-	action	________
ad-	adversary	________
ambi-	ambidextrous	________
ap-	application	________
ate-	cooperate	________
auto-	autonomous	________
circum-	circumnavigate	________
co-	cooperate	________
con-	construction	________

Prefix	Example	Example
de-	deface	______________
dis-	dissect	______________
e-	effervescent	______________
ed-	dedicated	______________
ex-	exclusion	______________
hypo-	hypodermic	______________
in-	instruct	______________
inter-	interface	______________
intro-	introspective	______________
mono-	monolith	______________
neo-	Neolithic	______________
per-	perennial	______________
pre-	preclude	______________
re-	reclaim	______________
retro-	retroactive	______________
trans-	transferable	______________

Suffixes

A suffix appears at the end of a word and changes the meaning of a word as well as its part of speech. For instance, the base word *ameliorate* (to improve) is a verb that can be changed slightly by dropping the *-e* and adding the suffix *-or* to create the noun *ameliorator* (one who improves) or *–ive* to create the word *ameliorative* (improving) or *-ion* to create the noun *amelioration* (improvement).

EXAMPLE Many suffixes are used in specialized academic vocabulary. By learning the meanings of the roots and suffixes, you can determine the definitions of many other words. For example, consider the suffix *-logy,* which means *science* or *study.* Many prefixes and roots can be added to this one suffix to indicate a plethora of other words. Use your dictionary to determine the definitions of the words below.

1. anthropology: study of the origins and customs of humanity

2. bacteriology: science of dealing with the study of bacteria

3. cardiology: science of the heart and its diseases

4. ecology: study of the environment

5. genealogy: study of the ancestry of a person or family

6. meteorology: science of the atmosphere and weather

7. mythology: study of myths

8. neurology: study of the nervous system and its diseases

9. paleontology: study of fossils and how they relate to life in the past

10. physiology: science of the functions of living things and their organs

11. sociology: study of human society

12. theology: study of religion and religious ideas

EXPLANATION You will notice that all of the words are nouns. You can change the part of speech, however, by changing *-logy* to *-logical,* which will then make each word an adjective. Furthermore, if you drop the letter *y* and add *-ist,* you then have the noun indicating the person who specializes in the field. Thus, you have changed the meaning.

EXERCISE 1 Suffixes

Study the following words and their definitions to determine the definition of each suffix.

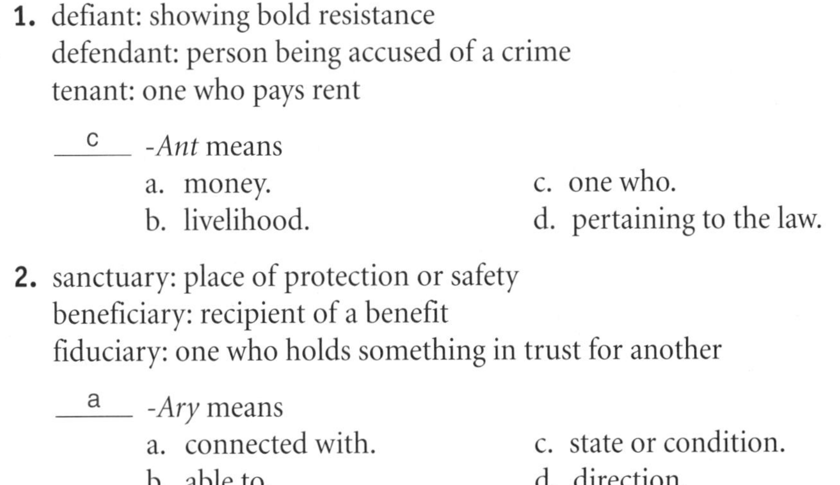

1. defiant: showing bold resistance
defendant: person being accused of a crime
tenant: one who pays rent

c *-Ant* means
a. money.
b. livelihood.
c. one who.
d. pertaining to the law.

2. sanctuary: place of protection or safety
beneficiary: recipient of a benefit
fiduciary: one who holds something in trust for another

a *-Ary* means
a. connected with.
b. able to.
c. state or condition.
d. direction.

3. fervent: showing great passion
silent: making no sound
solvent: able to pay one's debts

__c__ *-Ent* means
a. resembling; like.
b. in a certain manner.
c. that which shows.
d. in a certain direction.

4. phosphorescent: characterized by giving off light after exposure to radiant energy
effervescent: giving off bubbles; lively
evanescent: tending to fade

__c__ *-Escent* means
a. full of.
b. state; condition.
c. beginning to be.
d. one who does.

5. pragmatic: practical
ecstatic: very happy
hyperbolic: exaggerated

__d__ *-Ic* means
a. state; condition.
b. less.
c. full of.
d. like; being.

6. promotion: state of advancement in rank or position
aversion: condition of being in opposition
seclusion: condition of being alone

__a__ *-Ion* means
a. condition; state.
b. full of.
c. like.
d. expert.

7. rigorous: full of hardship
tenuous: lacking substance; flimsy
ponderous: heavy

__d__ *-Ous* means
a. condition; state.
b. make.
c. in the direction of.
d. full of.

8. inure: make accustomed to something painful
tenure: status of holding a permanent position
composure: state of calmness

__d__ *-Ure* means
a. resembling.
b. full of.
c. characteristic of.
d. state of

9. complexity: condition of being intricate and complicated
anonymity: state of being unknown
diversity: variety

__c__ *-Ity* means
a. resembling.
b. like; related to.
c. state; quality.
d. one who does something.

10. anatomy: dissection of plants and animals to determine their structure
dichotomy: cutting into two; division
phlebotomy: cutting a vein to diminish the blood supply

__b__ *-Tomy* means
a. study or science of.
b. cut.
c. account.
d. cause to become.

EXERCISE 2 Suffixes

Study the chart below and insert a second example of a word that contains each suffix and then its part of speech. You may need to consult a dictionary as well as the appendix in this book. (Answers will vary.)

Suffixes Guide

Suffix	Example	Example	Part of Speech
-able	valuable	______	adjective
-acle	spectacle	______	noun
-ade	facade	______	noun
-age	appendage	______	noun
-al	focal	______	adjective
-an	vegetarian	______	noun
-ant	claimant	______	noun
-ar	similar	______	adjective
-ary	dispensary	______	noun
-ate	investigate	______	verb
-ation	simulation	______	noun
-cide	genocide	______	noun
-e	simile	______	noun

Suffix	Example	Example	Part of Speech
-ed	studied	__________	verb
-ent	fervent	__________	adjective
-er	teacher	__________	noun
-erous	ponderous	__________	adjective
-escent	effervescent	__________	adjective
-ful	beautiful	__________	adjective
-gen	pathogen	__________	noun
-i	stimuli	__________	noun
-ic	historic	__________	adjective
-ical	comical	__________	adjective
-ile	infantile	__________	adjective
-ion	occasion	__________	noun
-is	epidermis	__________	noun
-ism	patriotism	__________	noun
-ist	nutritionist	__________	noun
-ition	nutrition	__________	noun
-ity	biodiversity	__________	noun
-ive	reclusive	__________	adjective
-less	penniless	__________	adjective
-ly	sensitively	__________	adverb
-ment	establishment	__________	noun
-nal	maternal	__________	adjective
-oid	steroid	__________	noun
-ology	microbiology	__________	noun
-or	author	__________	noun
-ous	dexterous	__________	adjective
-tion	vacation	__________	noun
-sis	analysis	__________	noun
-ure	juncture	__________	noun
-y	autonomy	__________	noun

Analogies

Analogies are word relationships that require critical thinking. The pairs of words are like puzzles that require the reader to determine the relationship presented. For example, daughter : girl : : son : boy. You would read this analogy as, "Daughter is to girl as son is to boy." Note that the first step is to make sure you know the definitions of all of the words. Next, you determine the relationship presented.

Analogies can present several kinds of relationships.

- Synonym (kind : nice :: unfriendly : mean).
- Antonym (friendly : mean :: heavy : light).
- A descriptive relationship (strong : wrestler :: tall : skyscraper).
- The relationship of the part to a whole (leg : body :: tire : car).
- The relationship of an item to a category (cabin : dwelling :: painting : art).

EXERCISE 1 Synonyms and Antonyms

Step 1: Determine the definitions and part of speech of each of the pairs presented.
Step 2: Determine the relationship of the first pair.
Step 3: Select the letter of the answer that completes the second pair with the same relationship as the first pair.

1. stalwart : advocate :: antagonist : a ____________
a. enemy b. supporter c. follower

2. lethargy : exhaustion :: lassitude : c ____________
a. exhilaration b. avoidance c. weariness

3. intrepid : afraid :: temerity : c ____________
a. relief b. forgetfulness c. reticence

4. glutton : food :: spendthrift : a ____________
a. money b. work c. banquet

5. egregious : obvious :: banal : a ____________
a. commonplace b. unique c. creative

6. mischievous : impish :: naughty : c ____________
a. expensive b. overbooked c. bad

7. lamentation : grief :: euphoria : b __________
   a. music   b. joy   c. sadness

8. feral : tame :: alleviate : c __________
   a. ease   b. praise   c. exacerbate

9. quell : soothe :: pacify : b __________
   a. intensify   b. mollify   c. exhaust

10. staid : silly :: outrageous : a __________
    a. boring   b. fun-loving   c. afraid

EXERCISE 2 Descriptive, Part to Whole, Item to Category

1. diligence : goal :: training : a __________
   a. championship   b. running   c. nutrition
2. rebel : autonomy :: immigrant : c __________
   a. memory   b. homeland   c. citizenship
3. surfing : waves :: hiking : c __________
   a. lake   b. movie   c. trail
4. chimichanga : flavorful :: blueberry pie : b __________
   a. hot   b. sweet   c. spicy
5. archer : precise :: figure skater : c __________
   a. awkward   b. sluggish   c. graceful
6. freshman : college :: Marine recruit : b __________
   a. university   b. boot camp   c. capitol
7. surgeon : scalpels :: painter : b __________
   a. museum   b. brushes   c. sculpture
8. string : guitar :: reed : c __________
   a. flute   b. drum   c. clarinet
9. submarine : ocean :: subway : c __________
   a. train   b. building   c. city
10. lexicon : word :: company : a __________
    a. employee   b. erasure   c. customer

Stop and Think

Read the following passage from a college history textbook and use context clues to select the best word from the box to fill in the blanks.

boundaries	esteemed	immortal	judges	sacrifices
dwelled	groves	instructed	priests	veneration

Julius Caesar, who conquered the Celtic tribes of Gaul, observed of the Celts that there were among them only two classes of people who counted: the warriors and the priests. The **(1)** priests, who were called Druids, taught that the human soul was **(2)** immortal and at death passed from one person to another. They also taught that spirits, many of them evil, **(3)** dwelled in forests, streams, springs, and rocks. They held the mistletoe in particular **(4)** veneration and chose **(5)** groves of oak as their special retreat. To protect those who were going into battle or to help those we were ill, they offered human **(6)** sacrifices. The Druids were more than priests; they were also physicians, teachers, prophets, and **(7)** judges. They taught young people their magic lore and they were judges in matters of crime and disputed **(8)** boundaries. Powerful and **(9)** esteemed, they counseled kings and **(10)** instructed the people.

—Clayton Roberts, David Roberts, & Douglas R. Bisson, A History of England, Vol. 1, 4th ed., Prentice-Hall, 2002, p. 16.

Visit the following Websites for more practice with context clues and word parts.

http://wps.ablongman.com/long_licklider_vocabulary_1/0,1682,11668-,00.html

http://wps.ablongman.com/long_licklider_vocabulary_1/0,1682,11839-,00.html

CHAPTER 2

Dictionary Skills

Get Ready to Read About Dictionary Skills

A good collegiate dictionary and thesaurus are important tools for a college student. Learning to use all of the features of the dictionary enhances your communication—both oral and written. As you prepare to read this chapter, think about what you know about the type of the information a dictionary, a thesaurus, and a glossary provide. Also, think about ways you can use these tools when preparing for classes and writing research papers.

Linguists are people who study language. They consider the origins of words as well as how language changes because it is dynamic and constantly evolving. For example, you are familiar with the word *lifestyle,* which means *a way of life.* However, the word first appeared in 1929 and finally became an accepted part of the American vocabulary in the early 1960s. Some words are created and added to dictionaries each year based on the frequency with which they are used. Likewise, as they become outdated, words are eliminated or labeled *archaic* or *obsolete,* which means they are no longer in common use. A treasure chest of information, a current collegiate dictionary is an essential tool for every college student.

Consider the following features of most dictionaries:

- Guide Words (the words at the top of each page)
- Spelling (how the word and its different forms are spelled)
- Syllabication (the word divided into syllables)
- Pronunciation (how to say the word)
- Part of speech (the function of the word)

- Definition (the meaning of the word, with the most common meaning listed first)
- Synonyms (words that have similar meaning)
- Etymology (the history of the word)

VISUAL VOCABULARY

The English teacher wants to destroy the billboard because the word irregardless is incorrect and should be regardless instead. (You may need to use a dictionary.)

Mark Parisi/off the mark.com

As you can see from the previous example, dictionaries also provide information about the correct usage of certain words that often cause confusion.

A rich vocabulary is closely related to academic success because it is linked to reading comprehension and writing skills. College students who want to succeed academically recognize that developing a strong vocabulary is an ongoing process that enhances their oral and written communication. Learning to use the tools of a dictionary, thesaurus, and glossary will augment vocabulary development.

Dictionary Entries

Spelling and Syllables

The spelling of the word is first given in bold type. In addition, the word is divided into syllables. A syllable is a unit of sound, and it includes one vowel sound. For instance, the word *read* has two vowels, *e* and *a*, but only one vowel sound, which is a long *e*.

In words with more than one syllable, the stress marks that indicate the syllables that are emphasized will guide you in the proper pronunciation of the word.

Note: Often, adding a suffix can change the stress and thus the pronunciation of a word.

EXAMPLE *prefer* (prĭ-fûr′) *preferable* (prĕf′ər-ə-bəl)
compare (kəm-pâr′) *comparable* (kŏm′pər-bəl)

EXPLANATION *Prefer* has two syllables. The second syllable is stressed more than the first, which is apparent because of the primary stress mark after the letter *r.* Now note how the stress mark changes for the word *preferable,* which has four syllables. The first syllable is now the one that is stressed more than the other three syllables. Likewise, the word *compare* has the primary stress on the last syllable. However, when the suffix *-able* is added, the primary stress moves to the first syllable of *comparable,* thus altering the pronunciation. As you can see, learning to read the symbols in a dictionary entry will help you communicate more effectively, and noting the stress marks is critical to pronouncing words correctly. For this reason, dictionaries contain a pronunciation key.

Pronunciation Symbols

Cover the right side of the page below, and then study the words at the left. Say each word without consulting a pronunciation guide. Uncover the pronunciations to check how you said the word. If you need more help, look at the chart on the next page. Note that several of the words presented are often mispronounced or have multiple pronunciations—all of which are considered correct.

1. caramel	(kăr′ə-məl, -mĕl′, kär′məl)
2. comparable	(kŏm′pər-ə-bəl)
3. consortium	(kən-sôr′tē-əm, -shē-əm)
4. mischievous	(mĭs′zhə-vəs)
5. segue	(sĕg′-wā′, sā′-gwā′)

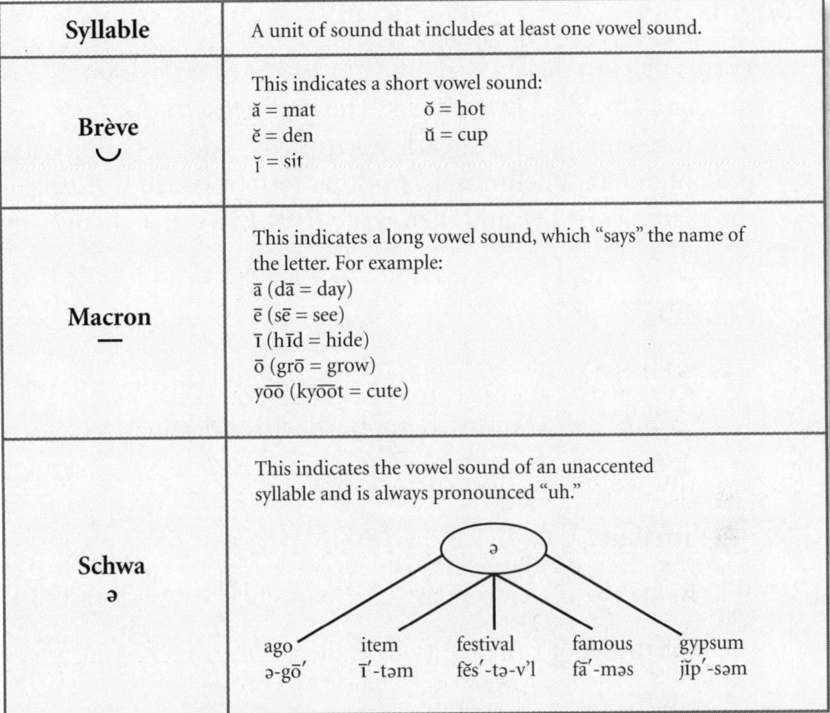

Syllable	A unit of sound that includes at least one vowel sound.
Brève ◡	This indicates a short vowel sound: ă = mat ŏ = hot ĕ = den ŭ = cup ĭ = sit
Macron —	This indicates a long vowel sound, which "says" the name of the letter. For example: ā (dā = day) ē (sē = see) ī (hīd = hide) ō (grō = grow) yo͞o (kyo͞ot = cute)
Schwa ə	This indicates the vowel sound of an unaccented syllable and is always pronounced "uh." ə ago ə-gō′ item ī′-təm festival fĕs′-tə-v′l famous fā′-məs gypsum jĭp′-səm

EXERCISE Pronunciation Symbols

Apply your understanding of phonetic symbols to decode the following quotations.

1. "Ōn′lē thə ĕj′-yo͞o-ka-tud är frē."—Epictetus

   "Only the educated are free."—Epictetus

2. "Hōld făst to͞o drēmz, fôr ĭf drēmz dī, līf ĭz ə brō′kən wĭngd bûrd *th*ăt kăn′ŏt flī."—Langston Hughes

   "Hold fast to dreams, for if dreams die, life is a broken winged bird that

   cannot fly."—Langston Hughes

3. "Thə fīr′wûrks′ bĭ-gĭn′ tə-dā′. Ēch dĭ-plō′mə ĭz ə līt′-ĭd măch. Ēch wŭn ŭv yo͞o ĭz ə fyo͞oz."—Ed Koch

   "The fireworks begin today. Each diploma is a lighted match. Each one

   of you is a fuse."—Ed Koch

Heteronyms

Words that are spelled the same but have a slightly different pronunciation and meaning are called *heteronyms.* The prefix *hetero-* means *different* and the root *nym* means *name;* thus, each heteronym indicates words that look alike but present different definitions. Another term for such words is *homograph.* Study the examples below, and then write what you think changes the pronunciation of each word.

EXAMPLE

1. **address**

   (ə-drĕs′) v. to speak to; to mark with a destination ________________

   (ăd′rĕs) n. location; formal speech ________________

2. **attribute**

   (ə-trĭb′yo͞ot) v. to relate to a particular cause; to ascribe ________________

   (ăt′rə-byo͞ot′) n. quality or trait ________________

3. **conflict**

   (kən-flĭkt′) v. to differ ________________

   (kŏn′flĭkt′) n. battle; disagreement________________

4. **contract**

   (kən-trăkt′) v. to establish by formal agreement ________________

   (kŏn′trăkt′) n. a written agreement ________________

5. **desert**

   (dĭ-zûrt′) v. to abandon ________________

   (dĕz′ərt) n. a dry, often sandy region; a wasteland ________________

6. **escort**

   (ĭ-skôrt′) v. to accompany ________________

   (ĕs′kôrt) n. one or more persons accompanying another to guide or show honor________________

EXPLANATION For the verbs, the primary stress is on the second syllable, and the first syllable is unstressed. For the nouns, the primary stress is on the first syllable.

Definitions

Dictionary entries usually have more than one meaning, so the definitions will be numbered, followed by the part of speech. The definition will sometimes be accompanied by a sentence of explanation of usage to clarify each meaning.

Study the dictionary entry below.

> [1]**sail** \sāl, *as last element in compounds often* səl\n. [ME,fr. OE *sgl;* akin to OHG *segal* sail] (bef. 12c) **1a** (1): an extent of fabric (as canvas) by means of which wind is used to propel a ship through water **b** pl *usu* **sail:** a ship equipped with sail **2:** an extent of fabric used to propelling a wind-driven vehicle (as an iceboat) **3:** something that resembles a sail; *esp.* : a streamlined conning tower on a submarine **4:** a passage by a sailing craft : cruise –sailed \'sāld\ adj—under sail : in motion with sails set **sail** *vi* (bef. 12c) **5a:** to travel on water in a ship **b:** YACHT **6:** to travel on water by the action of wind upon sails or by other means **7:** to move or proceed easily, gracefully, nonchalantly, or without resistance <~s through all sorts of contradictions—Vicki Hearne> <the bill ~ed through the legislature> **c:** to move through the air <the ball ~ed over his head>

—By permission. From *Merriam-Webster's Collegiate® Dictionary, Eleventh Edition*
© 2006 by Merriam-Webster, Incorporated (www.Merriam-Webster.com)

Multiple Meanings and Context Clues

To determine which of the multiple meanings you should use, apply what you have learned about context clues. Knowing how to recognize the parts of speech will also be a guide to the appropriate definition.

EXAMPLE Study the dictionary excerpt for *sail,* then select the number of the definition that best fits its use in the sentences below.

5a **1.** We will sail to Bermuda early in September on our first cruise ship voyage.

1a **2.** There was too much wind to raise the sails.

7 **3.** David sailed through his final exams without any trouble.

EXPLANATION

1. They will travel over water by ship.
2. They are in a sailboat with canvas sails.
3. David eased through the exams with little trouble or resistance

Connotation and Denotation

To communicate effectively, you will recognize that many words have a denotation as well as a connotation. **Denotation** means the dictionary definition. **Connotation** means the implied, or suggested, meaning. Furthermore, some words may have a positive connotation or a negative connotation. Think about the words *lie* and *embellish.* Although both can mean stretching the truth, *to lie* sounds much more evil than *to embellish the truth.* Another example is using the word *liberate* to mean *steal.* A savvy lawyer may use words with a positive connotation to sway a jury's opinion, and the word *liberate* implies freedom and patriotism—noble ideals—while the word *steal* implies something illegal. These words with positive connotations are also called **euphemisms.** A euphemism is a word that sounds good that replaces something that sounds less pleasing. In fact, the prefix *eu-* means *good,* and the root *phem* comes from the Greek root *phon,* which means *sound.* Another example of a euphemism, or word with a positive connotation, is "called to rest," which is used in place of the word "died," which signifies something final and less pleasing to hear.

Marketing strategies often involve recognizing the power of language and the use of euphemism. For example, because of the positive connotation of *cottage,* you would use that term, rather than *small house* if you were a realtor because the first term sounds charming, whereas the second sounds cramped. Likewise, as a jeweler, you might market a *delicately styled diamond* rather than a *small* one. The first description focuses on something *dainty* and *refined* rather than *tiny* and *cheap.*

Finally, another venue for using words with positive connotation is in government documents in which **propaganda** uses language to persuade and manipulate thinking. The propaganda often contains words with positive connotations, or euphemisms. Propaganda is a means by which an idea is widely spread. The word *propaganda,* first used by Pope Gregory XV, comes from a Latin term that means to *propagate* or *spread.* In 1612, the Pope created a department within the church to spread the Christian faith throughout the world by missionary work. Centuries later, President Woodrow Wilson used propaganda to sway the American people to enter World War I.

—Adapted: Henry, D.J. *The Master Reader*

Whether it is a marketing technique or government propaganda, college students learn the power of words and how language can shape their thinking and thus affect their actions.

EXAMPLE Check the statement that has a positive connotation (sounds more appealing).

✓ The state legislature has voted to add several fees to continue quality services for all residents.

______ The state legislature has voted to raise taxes for the coming year.

EXPLANATION Finding money to fund state projects is always a problem. Many legislators promise not to raise taxes, so the term always has a negative connotation. However, if you call the tax a *fee* instead, it is easier to pass on to the voters and will arouse less protest.

EXERCISE

Insert the letter of the wording with the more positive connotation.

1. The young high school students have applied to be servers at Eagle Harbor, a facility for b.
a. old people b. senior citizens

2. The new program will provide a safe haven each night during the winter months for those in the local area who are considered b.
a. vagrants b. homeless

3. Following the well-planned, top-secret air strikes, the journalists reported that the area sustained a great deal of b.
a. civilian casualties b. collateral damage

Etymology

Dictionary entries often begin with a history, or etymology, of the word. This information reveals the origin of the word and its meaning as well as how the connotation may have changed.

Sometimes the etymology involves word parts such as a prefix, root, or suffix. For other words, the etymology is connected to stories that provide a framework for the word. Often, knowing the story helps you remember the definition of the word. Study the following example from Greek mythology.

LABYRINTH

The word *labyrinth* comes from the Greek myth about King Minos of Crete and the minotaur, his son who was half man and half bull. According to legend, King Minos commissioned Daedalus to design an intricate maze, the Labyrinth, that would house the beast. There, young men and women would be led to their death because they could not find their way through the complex passages to freedom. Today the word *labyrinth* signifies a puzzle or maze.

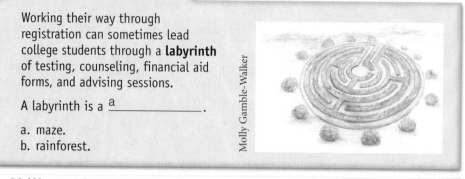

VISUAL VOCABULARY

Working their way through registration can sometimes lead college students through a **labyrinth** of testing, counseling, financial aid forms, and advising sessions.

A labyrinth is a a__________.

a. maze.
b. rainforest.

Molly Gamble-Walker

Dictionary Skills Review

Read the following story, and underline each time you see the word *draft* appear in the passage.

A CALL FOR MYSTERY

Jason struggled to stay focused on the calculus problem, but memories of the night before distracted him. Thinking about the woman he met at the homecoming dance brought a smile to his face—even in the solitude of the library.

They met near the end of the dance, but even at their introduction, there was something familiar about her he couldn't identify. For the rest of the evening, they enjoyed several songs, danced, and talked. Never had he felt so comfortable with a woman. Then, before he knew it, she was gone as mysteriously as she had appeared. But he could still see her in his mind—tousled brown hair piled on her head and a sleek red dress. There was also a mischievous, enigmatic look in her eyes. Just before she vanished, she had whispered, "Talk to you soon." But then she was gone.

Crazy. He did not even get her name. He had thought there would be time later for that. How was he supposed to find her now? It had only been a week, but the memory of the evening continued to haunt him. And the idea that she continued to distract him in her absence was incomprehensible. He was a scientist, not a romantic.

Jason stretched and then decided a walk around the library would help clear his head.

He wandered the stacks and ended up near a student lounge area by the front entrance, where he picked up a school newspaper. Skimming the headlines, he noticed her photo. She looked different. The hair was around her face, tumbled over her shoulders, but it was her photograph accompanying the column, and she wore a mischievous, mysterious grin. The name, though, was obviously a pseudonym: Ms. Tree.

Jason's heart leapt, however, as he read the column. Maybe he wasn't a romantic, but the scientist in him knew clues when he saw them, and this column was definitely a treasure trove of clues—all designed for Jason to discern the phone number of his mystery woman.

WHAT IS IT ABOUT A MAN?

A man can expertly call the plays in football,
And call the ball in the pocket at a pool hall.
He can call brothers to order in a fraternity meeting
And call those same friends by nicknames in a secret greeting.
He can call runners out at home plate,
And he can call a poker player's bluff with a straight.
If called for jury duty, he can show up on time,
And at a country dance, he can be called to stay in a line.
But when a woman says, "Call me," she generates confusion,
And as a result, the young man is suddenly cruisin'.
This is the first and last time I will call, but from the rooftops I'm summoning you,
And I look forward to hearing from you only if you're genuine and true.

You Are the Detective

To figure out the phone number of Ms. Tree, determine the number of the dictionary definition that corresponded to each context of the word *call.*

call \kôl\ *vt.* [ME. *callen* <Late OE. Ceallian & (or<) ON.*kalla* <IE. Base *gal-, to scream, shriek, whence Cym. galw, call, G. klage] **1.** to say or read in a loud tone; shout; announce [to call the names of stations] **2.** Sports to declare officially to be [the umpire called him out] **3.** a) in pool, to describe (the shot one plans to make) b) to predict **4.** to convoke judicially or officially [to call a meeting] **5.** to give or apply a name to [call the baby Ann] **6.** a) Poker to require (a player) to show his hand by equaling his bet b) to challenge on, or force to account for, something said or done c) to expose (someone's bluff) by such action **7.** to communicate with by telephone **8.** to summon to a specific duty, profession, etc. [the army called him] **9.** to utter or chant directions for (a square dance) ***10.** to stop or halt [game called because of rain] **11.** to demand or order payment of (a loan or bond issue) **12.** to imitate the sounds of in order to attract (a bird or animal) **13.** to command or ask to come; summon [call him to supper] **14.** to awaken [call me at six] **15.** to consider or describe as specified [I call it silly] **16.** to give orders for [to call a strike]

—From Webster's New World Dictionary, 2e by Editors of Webster's New World Dictionaries, Charlton Laird.

Step 1: Underline each instance of the word or form of the word *call* and determine the context that corresponds the definitions in the dictionary excerpt.
Step 2: Write the number of each definition that corresponds to the context in the letter. Ms. Tree's phone number is 9 3 4 - 5 2 6 - 8 9 7 1

Stop and Think

Go to **www.dictionary.reference.com, www.thesaurus.reference.com,** and **www.etymonline.com** to view online resources for the word *circadian* and then answer the following:

1. Which one provides the phonetic spelling of a word? dictionary.com
2. Which one provides the part of speech for the word? dictionary.reference .com and thesaurus.reference.com
3. Which one provides synonyms? thesaurus.reference.com
4. Which one provides antonyms? thesaurus.reference.com
5. Which one provides the history of the word? dictionary.reference.com and thesaurus.reference.com

✓ Use a dictionary to determine the definitions of the words found in the comic, and then summarize its content on your own paper.

Dan Piraro - 5.7.05/www.bizarro.com/King Features Syndicate

1. pedantic—narrow-mindedness; arbitrary
2. contrived—not natural or spontaneous enough
3. subsequent—next; following
4. altruistic—unselfish
5. enables—makes possible
6. transcend—rise above
7. quotidian—occurring every day
8. rhetoric—written composition

Review Test
Chapters 1–2

1 Word Parts

Match the definitions in Column 2 to the word parts in Column 1.

Column 1		Column 2
g	**1.** eco	a. make; do
d	**2.** path	b. cut
p	**3.** junct	c. foot
l	**4.** bio	d. feeling
n	**5.** trans-	e. call; cry out
q	**6.** poly-	f. same
m	**7.** ambi-	g. environment
o	**8.** -ary	h. love
t	**9.** log	i. around
s	**10.** -ous	j. beginning to be
h	**11.** phil	k. new
r	**12.** -ize	l. life
b	**13.** -tomy	m. both
j	**14.** -escent	n. across; change
i	**15.** peri	o. connected with
a	**16.** fac	p. join

1

f	**17.** sym-	q. many
k	**18.** neo	r. make; cause
c	**19.** pod	s. full of; resembling
e	**20.** claim, clam	t. word

2 Context Clues

Using context clues, select the letter of the best definition of the word in **bold** print.

1. Instead of continuous success, we only had **sporadic** victories with our new investment strategy.

c **Sporadic** means
a. constant. b. creative. c. periodic. d. regular.

2. For some, being organized is an **innate** quality; for others, it is a trait that must be developed.

a **Innate** means
a. natural. b. surprising. c. developed. d. learned.

3. From the balcony of the hilltop hotel, we enjoyed a beautiful vista of the beach and the cool **zephyr** that blew across the Caribbean Sea.

d **Zephyr** means
a. difficult climb. c. enthusiastic service.
b. attractive flowers. d. gentle wind.

4. The new supervisor expected everyone to be **obsequious** and obedient, so he was surprised to discover the employees had their own ideas of how to improve productivity.

b **Obsequious** means
a. assertive. c. unflattering.
b. submissive. d. unsure.

5. Rafting along the lazy river inspired and **enthralled** us as we identified eagles, ospreys, and ancient rock drawings from Indian vision quests of long ago.

c **Enthrall** means
a. persuade. b. permit. c. fascinate. d. calm.

6. After each shift of riding either the ambulance or the fire engine, Paul **regales** us with his stories of heroism and compassion.

__a__ **Regales** means
a. entertain. b. bore. c. avoid. d. ignore.

7. In spite of their poverty, their mother insisted on **decorous** behavior that included proper etiquette, correct grammar, and appropriate table manners.

__d__ **Decorous** means
a. awkward.
b. romantic.
c. impolite.
d. well-mannered.

8. The city manager was **adamant** about lowering taxes by a few cents, but he was also just as stubborn about raising property assessments by 25 percent.

__c__ **Adamant** means
a. unsure. b. polite. c. stubborn. d. decent.

9. Dean Smith is an excellent leader who encourages us to seek solutions to the major concerns and not to fret over the **inconsequential** ones.

__b__ **Inconsequential** means
a. large. b. trivial. c. major. d. important.

10. After a quick vote, it was clear that everyone **acceded** to the proposal, and such complete agreement was a sign of their future success.

__b__ **Accede** means
a. free. b. agree. c. find. d. reject.

3 Context Clues and Word Parts

Step 1: Identify the type of context clue presented in the sentence and underline the word(s) you used to determine the definition of the word in **bold** print; then write the definition of the word part(s).
Step 2: Select the letter of the definition of the word.

1. The essay was so **ambiguous** and confusing that Lori's teacher told her she would have to redo the paper.

Context Clue: synonym Word Parts: *ambi*: both;
-ous: resembling; full of

__b__ **Ambiguous** means
a. insightful. b. unclear. c. clear. d. agreeable.

1

2. Instead of kindness, he felt only **antipathy** for his co-workers, which prompted him to prepare his résumé and apply for a new job.

Context Clue: antonym Word Parts: *anti-*: against; *pathy*: feeling

a **Antipathy** means
a. hatred. b. friendship. c. popularity. d. respect.

3. Spenser had been a **bibliophile** for many years, and now his collection of first editions could fill a small library.

Context Clue: general context Word Parts: *biblio*: book; *phil*: love

d **Bibliophile** means
a. lover of the Bible.
b. list of sources.
c. lover of biographies.
d. lover of books.

4. Sara decided to join the newspaper staff instead of a campus organization that could exclude others and **circumscribe** whom she could choose to associate with or how she could spend her free time.

Context Clue: general context Word Parts: *circum-*: around; *scrib*: write

b **Circumscribe** means
a. view. b. restrict. c. study. d. accept.

5. Because of the atmosphere of **dissent** in the local political arena, the current candidate is hoping to eliminate that disagreement and generate a feeling of cooperation.

Context Clue: synonym Word Part: *dis-*: not; separated from

c **Dissent** means
a. consent.
b. consideration.
c. opposition.
d. agreement.

6. Because many students graduate within two years, a community college feels more **transient** than a four-year college, whose student body remains permanent twice as long.

Context Clue: antonym

Word Part: *trans-*: change; across

b **Transient** means
a. difficult.
b. temporary.
c. permanent.
d. unfair.

1

7. During the 1920s, the **interdict** to prohibit the production, sale, or consumption of alcoholic beverages proved impossible to enforce.

Context Clue: general context

Word Parts: *inter*: between; *dict*: speak; say

a **Interdict** means
- a. prohibition.
- b. law.
- c. permit.
- d. invention.

8. The captain's farewell **monologue** in the classic film The Ghost and Mrs. Muir is one of the most romantic speeches in film history.

Context Clue: synonym Word Parts: *mono*: one; *log*: word

b **Monologue** means
- a. conversation.
- b. speech by one.
- c. judgment.
- d. advertisement.

9. The **euphony** of the new chorus on campus is a joy to hear; in contrast, the harsh sounds of construction in the surrounding buildings make it difficult to enjoy.

Context Clue: antonym Word Parts: *eu*-: pleasing; *phon*: sound

b **Euphony** means
- a. harsh sound.
- b. rich melody.
- c. new sound.
- d. complication.

10. **Perinatal** procedures such as childcare instruction or the Lamaze childbirth method include important information for soon-to-be parents.

Context Clue: example Word Parts: *peri*-: around; *natal*-: birth

a **Perinatal** means
- a. around the time of a birth.
- b. after the time of a birth.
- c. during the time of a birth.
- d. education methods.

4 Phonetic Analysis

Write out the quotations that are spelled phonetically here.

1. "Hōp ĭz ə wā′kĭng drēm."—Aristotle

"Hope is a waking dream."—Aristotle

2. "Rēl sək-sĕs′ ĭz fīn′dĭng yo͞or līf′wûrk′ ĭn *th*ə work *th*ăt yo͞o lŭv."—David McCullough

"Real success is finding your lifework in the work that you love."—David McCullough

3. "Nŏt to͞o nō ĭz băd. Nŏt to͞o wŏnt to͞o nō ĭz wûrs. Nĭt to͞o hōp ĭz ŭn-thĭng′kə-bəl. Nŏt to͞o kâr ĭz ŭn′fər-gĭv′ə-bəl."—Nigerian Saying

"Not to know is bad. Not to want to know is worse. Not to hope is unthinkable. Not to care is unforgivable."—Nigerian Saying

4. "Dōnt bŏ*th*′ər jŭst to͞o bē bĕt′ər *th*ăn yo͞or kən-tĕm′pə-rĕ′rēz ôr prĕd′-ĭ-sĕs′ərs. Trī to͞o be bĕt′ər *th*ăn yo͞or-sĕlf′."—William Faulkner

"Don't bother just to be better than your contemporaries or predecessors. Try to be better than yourself."—William Faulkner

5. "Kēp ə-wā′ frŭm pē′pəl ho͞o trī to͞o bĭ-lĭt′l yo͞or ăm-bĭsh′əns. Smôl pē′pəl ôl′wāz do͞o *th*ăt, bŭt *th*ə rē′ə-lē′ grāt māk yo͞o fēl *th*ăt yo͞o, to͞o, kăn bĭ-kŭm′ grāt." —Mark Twain

"Keep away from people who try to belittle your ambitions. Small people always do that, but the really great make you feel that you, too, can become great."—Mark Twain

5 Dictionary Usage

Use your dictionary to answer the following questions.*

1. What is the first definition of the word *amenity*? The quality of being pleasant or agreeable.
2. What is the part of speech of the French term *au revoir*? noun
3. How many definitions are listed for the word *circle*? seven
4. How many syllables in the word *victual*? two
5. What does *victual* mean? n. food usable by people; vt. To eat

*Suggested answers are based on *Merriam-Webster's Collegiate Dictionary*, 11th ed.

6. What is a synonym for *victual*? provision

7. What year did the word *victual* appear as a verb? 1514

8. What consonant is silent in the word *victual*? C

9. What are four synonyms presented for *vigorous*? energetic; strenuous; lusty; nervous

10. What is one example presented as a use for *vigorous*? as vigorous as a youth half his age

UNIT 2 Vocabulary in Health, Nursing, and Science

CHAPTER 3 Vocabulary in Health

Get Ready to Read About Health

College health textbooks contain reading selections on a variety of subjects about physical, mental, and emotional well-being. In addition, you will encounter chapters about the environment as well as those dealing with physical and mental stress. In this selection, you will read about a topic on stress management, which concerns mental and emotional health. Before you read, consider what you already know about the following word parts. The meanings of some have been provided. Recall what you learned in Chapter 1 and fill in the blanks for the others.

1. The prefix *com-* means with, together.
2. The prefix *de-* means down, from, away.
3. The suffix *-ness* means *quality, state, condition*, and usually indicates a noun.
4. The suffix *-ous* means *like, related to, full of*, and usually indicates an adjective.
5. The suffix *-tion* means *action, state*, and usually indicates a noun.

aggression	anxious	comply	demean	modality
alienation	assertiveness	degradation	impasse	shrewd

ASSERTIVENESS

Verbal **assertiveness** is saying what you like or dislike about someone or something without using **degradation;** it is getting what you want but not at the expense of someone else's self-esteem. Assertiveness is "feel good" communication. Some people confuse assertiveness with **aggression.** Aggression is demanding in a bossy and **demeaning** way that someone obeys your wishes. It is an act of verbal pushing and shoving with no thought for the other person's self-esteem. When the other person does not **comply** or agree, the aggressor insists that he or she is "dumb," "stupid," or "crazy" for not agreeing. When people respond to a situation aggressively, they often receive counter-aggression, **alienation,** and defensiveness from the other person. Communication reaches an **impasse,** and all who are involved come away from the situation feeling **anxious,** angry, and misunderstood.

At the opposite end of the scale from aggression is nonassertive or passive behavior. Many have learned in childhood to be passive pleasers who do not have the skill to ask for what they want. Their **modality** of operation is to manipulate. They sit back wishing someone would notice their needs and fulfill them, or they set up **shrewd** and round-about ways of getting what they want. Manipulators use guilt to get others to do what they want. They control others with *shoulds, oughts,* and *ifs;* nonassertiveness is highly related to low self-concept. In becoming more assertive, it is important to know that you have certain inalienable assertive rights, which include the rights to do the following:

- say no without feeling guilty
- change your mind
- take your time in planning your answer
- ask for instructions or directions
- demand respect
- do less than you possibly can
- ask for what you want
- experience and express your feelings
- feel good about yourself, no matter what

—Adapted from Girdano, Everly, and Dusek, *Controlling Stress and Tension*, 6th ed., pp. 86–87.Reprinted with permission.

VISUAL VOCABULARY

Nervousness before a formal dance often causes a couple to feel a________.

a. anxious.
b. shrewd.

George Pongratz

EXERCISE 1 Context Clues

Refer to the previous passage and use context clues from the sentences below to determine the definition of each of the following words in **bold** print. Do not consult a dictionary.

1. aggression (ə-grĕsh′ən) n.
The **aggression** Sam expressed toward people who were different from him prompted his friends to feel that such destructive behavior was the result of his personal frustration and insecurity rather than strength.

__d__ **Aggression** means
a. strong leadership.
b. silent frustration.
c. passive or weak behavior.
d. hostile or forceful action.

2. alienation (āl′yə-nā′shən) n.
The isolation and **alienation** a person feels when grieving the loss of a loved one can be avoided if he or she has a supportive network of friends.

__a__ **Alienation** means
a. separation. b. grief. c. network. d. anger.

3. anxious (ăngk′shəs) adj.
Although Bobby was excited about attending an Ivy League school, he was also **anxious,** but he planned to summon his courage to overcome that sense of fear before orientation.

__b__ **Anxious** means
a. angry. b. concerned. c. poor. d. proud.

4. assertiveness (ə-sûr′tĭv-nĕs) n.
The **assertiveness** of the new president was projected in his confident manner as well as in his ability to laugh at himself.

__a__ **Assertiveness** means
a. bold self-assurance.
b. shyness.
c. extreme kindness.
d. seriousness.

5. comply (kəm-pl′ī) v.
"Failure to **comply** with our policies may result in your being dismissed from the college," explained the computer lab director, who was giving an orientation lecture.

__d__ **Comply** means
a. argue. b. oppose. c. disobey. d. adhere to.

6. degradation (dĕg′rə-dā′shən) n.
The **degradation** people have experienced in wartime prisons is a frightening reminder of the evil actions that people are capable of doing.

__d__ **Degradation** means
a. elevation.
b. advancement.
c. pride.
d. humiliation.

7. demean (dĭ-mēn′) v.
Comments that **demean** others such as references to someone's lack of education or good looks or personal wealth are often a sign of insecurity rather than high status.

__a__ **Demean** means
a. belittle. b. praise. c. organize. d. sensitize.

8. impasse (ĭm′păs′) n.
In spite of many hours of negotiations, by midnight both parties were still at an **impasse,** and that dead end prevented any hope of a settlement before dawn.

__c__ **Impasse** means
a. good fortune.
b. compromise.
c. barrier.
d. solution.

9. modality (mō-dăl′ĭ-tē) n.
The local police officers use a variety of **modalities** of transportation including unmarked cars, motorcycles, horses, bicycles, and Segways.

__a__ **Modality** means
a. manner. b. tradition. c. vehicle. d. veto.

10. shrewd (shro͞od) adj.
Dr. Rollins has a **shrewd** sense of humor that requires the listener to notice his crafty wit.

b **Shrewd** means
a. innocent. b. cunning. c. simple. d. easy.

EXERCISE 2 Word Sorts

Synonyms

Match the word to the synonyms or definitions that follow each blank.

1. comply obey; conform; acquiesce
2. degradation humiliation; demotion; downgrading
3. modality form; style; manner
4. impasse dead end; obstruction; barrier
5. shrewd crafty; artful; insidious

Antonyms

Select the letter of the word(s) with the opposite meaning.

a 6. demean
a. praise b. intervene c. obey d. humiliate

b 7. assertiveness
a. affirmation b. shyness c. boldness d. profession

b 8. aggression
a. hostility b. peacefulness c. attack d. interest

d 9. alienation
a. isolation b. wonder c. criticism d. inclusion

a 10. anxious
a. self-assured b. concerned c. sorrowful d. fearful

EXERCISE 3 Fill in the Blank

Use context clues to determine the word that best completes each sentence.

1. The modalities of communication have advanced quickly over the past few years with new features on cell phones, personal PDAs, MP3 players, Instant Messaging, and e-mail.

2. Films that display degradation ________ of people and animals usually carry a disclaimer to warn people of the offensive images, but critics feel such humiliation of life is always unjustified.

3. S.E. Hinton, author of several young adult novels, wrote her first book *The Outsiders* at the age of sixteen, just when she was experiencing some of the alienation ________ her characters depict.

4. Before signing the contract, Ben read the document carefully to ensure that he would be able to comply ________ with the requirements of the lease.

5. Although the criticism during the debate was not obviously crafty to most people in the audience, Glenn recognized the shrewd ________ attack on his integrity but chose, instead, to take the high road and only react compassionately to his opponent.

6. Because she had been raised to be a well-behaved and agreeable child who would never insist on her own way, Annie decided to read some self-help books on assertiveness ________ training such as *Play Like a Man, Win Like a Woman: What Men Know About Success That Women Need to Learn* by Gail Evans.

7. The leaders worked diligently on a compromise to avoid an impasse ________ because such a standoff could be disastrous to both countries.

8. Sitting outside the office, Joe suddenly began to feel anxious ________ about the interview, even though he had meticulously prepared for it for several days.

9. When the supervisor demeaned ________ Alexis in front of her customers and co-workers, she contained her humiliation and quietly went back to work, but she presented her two weeks' notice at the end of the day.

10. Some parenting authorities teach that spanking a child is a form of aggression ________ rather than discipline and can encourage children to develop a more hostile attitude toward others.

EXERCISE 4 Application

Using context clues, insert the vocabulary word in the appropriate blank. A part-of-speech clue is given for each vocabulary word.

After reading *The Lord of the Flies* by William Golding, you may have wondered how Jack and his followers could **(1)** (v.) demean Piggy with their comments of **(2)** (n.) degradation about his appearance or show overt **(3)** (n.) aggression toward Ralph or win the more vulnerable boys through **(4)** (adj.) shrewd trickery. The fictional story, however, mirrors a similar discovery made in a 1961 experiment by Yale psychologist Stanley Milgram, who directed participants to **(5)** (v.) comply with his orders to administer electric shock to other subjects in order to determine the effect of punishment on learning. At least that is what he told them. The real purpose of the experiment was to determine how much pain ordinary people were willing to inflict on others when ordered, no matter what the **(6)** (n.) modality of pain administration.

The results of the Milgram Experiment were surprising. Even when those receiving the jolts of electricity screamed in agony and the subjects administering the shock appeared **(7)** (adj.) anxious about their role, they did not stop.

People may reach an **(8)** (n.) impasse when debating the innate goodness of humans in comparison to their inherent evil. Instead of focusing on the negative results of the experiment, however, people should use the knowledge to encourage others to develop an **(9)** (n.) assertiveness —a bold confidence that allows them to say, "No, I will not do this because it is wrong." Thus, humanity will evolve and compassion will prevail.

The lessons of *Lord of the Flies* and the Milgram Experiment indicate that we do not live in isolation and should not cause others to experience **(10)** (n.) alienation. We are, instead, interconnected and dependent upon each other, not just for survival, but ultimately for the collective triumph of humankind.

Stop and Think

Using at least three words from the list, summarize the passage in 50 words or less. (Answers will vary.)

Assertiveness is a valued quality to develop since it promotes good communication and counters **aggression,** which is negatively exhibited in forms of **alienation** and **degradation,** making others **anxious** and thus causing an **impasse** in discussions. (35 words)

Study the images and write the vocabulary word that best summarizes each picture. Then write a sentence explaining your rationale. (Answers may vary.)

Courtesy of Microsoft.	1. anxious Biting fingernails is an example of body language exhibiting worry or fear.
Courtesy of Microsoft.	2. impasse The couple is fuming, and rather than solving their problem, they seem to be at a dead end in the discussion.
Courtesy of Microsoft.	3. alienation Locked in the bird cage, this office worker is isolated from everyone else.
Courtesy of Microsoft.	4. comply In this contract negotiation, one party has agreed to follow the requirements established by the other.
Courtesy of Microsoft.	5. aggression Because of their disagreement with the British crown, the colonists showed their aggression in Boston Harbor by making their own wishes known rather than allowing English oppression to continue.

CHAPTER 4 Vocabulary in Nursing Fundamentals

Get Ready to Read About Nursing Fundamentals

College textbooks for introductory nursing courses present topics on the fundamentals of individual, family, and community health. In this selection, you will read some of the basics about illness and disease. Before you read, consider what you already know about the following word parts. The meanings of some have been provided. Recall what you learned in Chapter 1 and fill in the blanks for the others.

1. The prefix *dis-* means not, separated from.
2. The prefix *ex-* means out, from, away.
3. The prefix *re-* means again.
4. The prefix *sub-* means under, below.
5. The root *chron* means *time, order*.
6. The root *ject* means *throw*.
7. The suffix *-ible* means *able to* and indicates an adjective.
8. The suffix *-ic* means *resembling, like* and indicates an adjective.
9. The suffix *-ology* means *study, science of* and indicates a noun.
10. The suffix *-tion* means *condition* and indicates a noun.

ameliorate	chronic	duration	exacerbation	subjective
causation	dissipate	etiology	remission	subside

ILLNESS AND DISEASE

Illness is a highly personal state in which the person's physical, emotional, intellectual, social, developmental, or spiritual functioning is thought to **dissipate.** It is not synonymous with disease and may not be related to disease. An individual could have a disease, for example, a growth in the stomach, and not feel ill. Similarly, a person can feel ill, that is, feel uncomfortable, yet have no discernible disease. Illness is highly **subjective;** only the individual can say he or she is ill.

Disease can be described as an alteration in body functions resulting in a reduction of capacities or a shortening of the normal life span. Traditionally, intervention by physicians has the goal of eliminating or **ameliorating** disease processes. Primitive people thought "forces" or spirits caused disease. Later this belief was replaced by the single-causation theory. Today multiple factors are considered to interact in causing disease and determining an individual's response to treatment.

The **causation** of disease is called its **etiology.** A description of the etiology of a disease includes the identification of all causal factors that act together to bring about the particular disease. There are, however, many diseases for which the cause is unknown (e.g. multiple sclerosis).

There are many ways to classify illness and disease; one of the most common is acute or **chronic.** Acute illness is typically characterized by severe symptoms of relatively short **duration.** The symptoms appear abruptly and **subside** quickly and, depending on the cause, may or may not require intervention by health care professionals.

A chronic illness is one that lasts for an extended period, usually 6 months or longer, and often for the person's life. Chronic illnesses usually have a slow onset and often have periods of **remission,** when the symptoms disappear, and **exacerbation,** when the symptoms reappear.

—Adapted from Kozier, Erb, Berman, and Snyder, *Fundamentals of Nursing,* 7th ed., p. 182. Prentice Hall. Reprinted with permission.

VISUAL VOCABULARY

Navy personnel who are in the community college's medical laboratory program form study groups and quiz each other on topics such as the ___a___, or origin of diseases.

a. etiology
b. remission

Susan Pongratz

EXERCISE 1 Context Clues

Refer to the previous passage and use context clues from the sentences below to determine the definition of each of the following words in **bold** print. Do not consult a dictionary.

1. ameliorate (ə-mēl′yə-rāt′) v.
Courageous people **ameliorate** problems, but cowards only make them worse.

___a___ **Ameliorate** means
a. fix. b. avoid. c. return. d. increase.

2. causation (kô-zā′shən) n.
Pondering the events of his life—the **causations** and the results—Tom said, "Everything happens for a reason."

___b___ **Causation** means
a. act or process of ignoring. c. regret.
b. act or process of causing. d. memory.

3. chronic (krŏn′ĭk) adj.
Matt's **chronic** absenteeism from his job resulted in his being dismissed after only six months of work.

___c___ **Chronic** means
a. crafty. b. unnoticed. c. continuing. d. rare.

4. dissipate (dĭs′ə-pāt′) v.
Mick sat counting his blessings and admitted that although he could find no reason for his sadness, his depression would not **dissipate.**

__b__ **Dissipate** means
a. unnoticed.
b. vanish.
c. hidden.
d. insignificant.

5. duration (do͞o-rā′shən) n.
Because of the **duration** of six months of shoulder pain, James realized he needed to see a doctor to determine if he needed surgery or physical therapy.

__d__ **Duration** means
a. unintentional. b. break. c. ease. d. length.

6. etiology (ē′tē-ŏl′ə-jē) n.
Despite extensive tests, Mary realized the doctors may never know the **etiology** of her disease, but they could still treat the symptoms.

__c__ **Etiology** means
a. study of medical tests.
b. science of pain management.
c. study of the cause of a disease.
d. symptom.

7. exacerbation (ĭg-zăs′ər-bā′shən) n.
Following your surgery, you will need your doctor's permission before you exercise to avoid **exacerbation** of the problem.

__a__ **Exacerbation** means
a. increase in severity.
b. decrease in severity.
c. permission.
d. relief.

8. remission (rĭ-mĭsh′ən) n.
After four chemotherapy treatments, Arline learned that her cancer was in **remission** and that her energy level would soon improve.

__b__ **Remission** means
a. an increase in severity.
b. a decrease in severity.
c. major concern.
d. central nervous system.

9. subjective (səb-jĕk′tĭv) adj.
Although there are always certain aspects to consider when evaluating a film, ultimately the decision of whether or not a movie is good is a **subjective** one.

b **Subjective** means
a. based on logic.
b. based on personal opinion.
c. specific.
d. well-supported.

10. subside (səb-sīd′) v.
After her weeping finally **subsided,** Allison realized the one man she loved the most was the one who had stood by her as her best friend for the past five years.

d **Subside** means
a. embarrass. b. excite. c. increase. d. decrease.

EXERCISE 2 Word Sorts

Synonyms

Match the word to the synonyms or definitions that follow each blank.

1. etiology study of the causes or origins of diseases
2. remission period in which symptoms of a disease decrease
3. exacerbation worsening; sharpening; intensifying
4. duration length; extent; period
5. chronic persisting; incessant; continuing

Antonyms

Select the letter of the word(s) with the opposite meaning.

c 6. causation
a. root b. origin c. effect d. satisfaction

a 7. ameliorate
a. damage b. improve c. fix d. adjust

c 8. dissipate
a. recognize b. clear c. gather d. failed

b 9. subjective
a. impulsive b. unbiased c. personal d. partial

d 10. subside
a. diminish b. wane c. recede d. increase

EXERCISE 3 Fill in the Blank

Use context clues to determine the word that best completes each sentence.

1. Although articles on the front page of the newspaper are factual and objective, those on the op-ed section are expected to be subjective______ because they include writers' opinions.

2. To ameliorate______ communication problems in a relationship, many couples try to learn active listening techniques.

3. In addition to treating symptoms, a doctor will try to identify the causation______ of an illness.

4. Medical interns in a problem-based learning curriculum take a course in etiology______, the study of the causes of diseases, to help them make the appropriate diagnoses.

5. Cancer survivors speak in terms of being in remission______ rather than of being cured, but the goal of cancer research is to extend lives and improve the quality of life of each patient.

6. Allison could give no reason for ending her relationship with Josh except that her interest in him had dissipate(d)______.

7. The chronic______ knee pain John experienced as a result of his jogging accident never eased up, no matter what efforts he made to relieve the ache.

8. Weather reports indicated that the storm winds had subside(d)______ and the hurricane had been downgraded to a tropical depression.

9. Although attempts to eliminate beach erosion were extensive, many of the techniques only exacerbate(d)______ rather than relieved the problem.

10. Bull riding, which is one rodeo sport, requires a rider to stay on a bull for a duration______ of at least eight seconds.

EXERCISE 4 Application

Using context clues, insert the vocabulary word in the appropriate blank. A part-of-speech clue is given for each vocabulary word.

Pain management is a discipline that continually concerns physicians. When health professionals can diagnose the **(1)** (n.) causation______ of discomfort, they can **(2)** (v.) ameliorate______, or relieve, the pain. At the same time, they recognize the sensation of pain is **(3)** (adj.) subjective________. That is, what may be manageable to one person may be unbearable to another.

Recognizing the two kinds of pain—acute and **(4)** (adj.) chronic________—is often part of the study of the origins of diseases, or **(5)** (n.) etiology________. Acute pain usually has a quick onset and may result from a discernible cause such as trauma, which is easily identified. Thus, symptoms usually **(6)** (v.) subside________ as soon as treatment begins. Chronic pain, on the other hand, may be more difficult to diagnose because of its longer **(7)** (n.) duration________ and the fact that **(8)** (n.) exacerbation________ of the pain will intensify if left untreated. This can be very frustrating to a patient.

Methods of pain management often incorporate myriad approaches, including pharmacological, non-pharmacological, and psychological approaches. In some cases, all of these treatments may be used to ease the patient into **(9)** (n.) remission________ from the pain if a definite cure cannot be attained. The goal of physicians is always to help the pain eventually **(10)** (v.) dissipate________, but if it does not vanish, then learning to manage the pain is the next goal.

Source: http://en.wikipedia.org/wiki/Pain_management

Stop and Think

Go to **www.etymonline.com** and search the words objective and subjective to complete the summary below.

1. objective

In 1620________, the word originally meant "considered in relation to its object" and was from the Latin word *ojectum*, which means "object." In 1855________, it was first used to mean "unbiased________." In 1738________ the noun was intended to mean "something objective to the mind." Not until near the end of the Civil War in 1864 was the word used to mean "goal, aim" when it was intended as a military term.

2. subjective

First appearing in 1315, the word meant "person under control or dominion of another" and had evolved from the Old French *suget, subget,* "a subject person or thing." The word originally came from the *Latin* prefix *sub-* meaning "under" and the root *jacere,* which means "to throw." In 1592, the word meant "person or thing that may be acted upon" and in 1541, it meant "subject matter of an art or science." The word *subjective,* meaning "existing in the mind," is from 1707.

—From www.etymonline.com. Copyright © 2006. Reprinted by permission of Douglas Harper.

Using your dictionary, write the definitions of the following words that include the root *chron,* which means *time* or *order.* You may also want to consult **www.etymonline.com** for examples.

1. anachronism: someone or something that is out of its proper or chronological order.
2. asynchronous: not occurring or existing at the exact time of occurrence. An example is asynchronous computer communication such as e-mail.
3. chronicle (n.): a collection of historical events
4. chronicle (v.): to record in the form of historical record
5. chronology: the order in which something happens
6. dendrochronology: The study of climate changes and past events by comparing the successive annual growth rings of trees or old timber. (www.dictionary.reference.com)
7. synchronic: occurring at the same time
8. synchronism: coincidence in time
9. synchronous: occurring at the same time; moving at the same rate
10. synchronize: to operate in unison

Vocabulary in Nursing Issues

Get Ready to Read About Nursing Issues

Nursing issues include many current events topics from prenatal care to euthanasia. In this selection, you will read about a growing field, patient advocacy. Before you read, consider what you already know about the following word parts. The meanings of some have been provided. Recall what you learned in Chapter 1 and fill in the blanks for the others.

1. The prefix *ad-* means to, toward ________.
2. The prefix *in-* means in, inside ________.
3. The root *dur* means *harden, last.*
4. The root *loc* means *place.*
5. The root *voc* means *call.*
6. The suffix *-acy* means *quality, state* and usually indicates a noun ________.
7. The suffix *-ent* means *like, related, of, being* and usually indicates an adjective ________.
8. The suffix *-tion* means action, process ________ and usually indicates a noun ________.
9. The suffix *-ate* means cause to become, make ________ and usually indicates a verb ________; however, in both contexts below, *surrogate* and *advocate* are nouns.

advocate	bureaucracy	incompetent	mediate	proxy
ascertain	convey	locus	mutual	surrogate

PATIENT ADVOCACY

When people are ill, they are frequently unable to assert their rights as they would if they were healthy. An **advocate** is one who expresses and defends the cause of another. A client advocate is an advocate for clients' rights. The health care system is complex and many clients are too ill to deal with it. If they are to keep from "falling through the cracks," clients need an advocate to cut through the layers of **bureaucracy** and help them get what they require. Clients may also advocate for themselves. Today, clients are seeking more self-determination and control over their own bodies when they are ill.

If a client lacks decision-making capacity, is legally **incompetent,** or is a minor, a patient's rights can be exercised on the client's behalf by a designated **surrogate** or **proxy,** or substitute decision maker. It is important, however, for the nurse to remember that client control over health decisions is a Western view. In other countries and societies, such decisions may normally be made by the head of the family or another member of the community. The nurse must **ascertain** the client and family's views and honor their traditions regarding the **locus** of decision making.

An advocate supports clients in their decisions, giving them full or at least **mutual** responsibility in decision making when they are capable of it. The advocate must be careful to remain objective and not **convey** approval or disapproval of the client's choices. Advocacy requires accepting and respecting the client's right to decide, even if the nurse believes the decision to be wrong.

In **mediating,** the advocate directly intervenes on the client's behalf, often by influencing others. An example of acting on behalf of a client is asking a physician to review with the client the reasons for and the expected duration of therapy because the client says he always forgets to ask the physician.

—Adapted from Kozier, Erb, and Snyder, *Fundamentals of Nursing,* 7th ed., p. 81. Prentice Hall. Reprinted with permission.

VISUAL VOCABULARY

Health professionals learn to a ______________ a patient's illness by diagnosing the symptoms.

a. ascertain
b. mediate

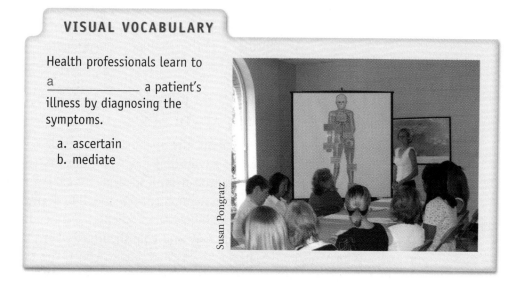

Susan Pongratz

EXERCISE 1 Context Clues

Refer to the previous passage and use context clues from the sentences below to determine the definition of each of the following words in **bold** print. Do not consult a dictionary.

1. advocate (ăd′və-kĭt) n.
After studying psychology and sociology in college, Sebastian volunteered to be a court-appointed special **advocate,** or CASA volunteer, to act on behalf of children without a network of support.

__a__ **Advocate** means
a. supporter. b. student. c. critic. d. politician.

2. ascertain (ăs′ər-tān′) v.
The CSI team ran a thorough investigation to **ascertain** the chain of events leading to the crime.

__d__ **Ascertain** means
a. praise. b. descend. c. resist. d. determine.

3. bureaucracy (byo͞o-rŏk′rə-sē) n.
Because of a web of **bureaucracy** in which little control was exercised, government spending exceeded reasonable amounts, and a new commission was formed to streamline the existing organization.

__b__ **Bureaucracy** means
a. journalistic privilege. c. recognition.
b. network of departments. d. leadership.

4. convey (kən-vā′) v.
To **convey** to her students the rhythm of iambic pentameter that Shakespeare used in his plays, Dr. Monaco compared the ten beats per line to the beating of their hearts.

__c__ **Convey** means
a. hide. b. test. c. express. d. receive.

5. incompetent (ĭn-kŏm′pĭ-tənt) adj.
The coach was relieved of his duties when the college board decided he was **incompetent** at leading the football team—their explanation for a series of 16 losses.

__a__ **Incompetent** means
a. not capable of doing good work.
b. unwilling to work.
c. not sensitive.
d. not comfortable.

6. locus (lō′kəs) n.
Every Sunday dinner was held at the grandparents' home, the **locus** of many family gatherings and happy memories.

__d__ **Locus** means
a. beginning.
b. border.
c. outer barrier.
d. central place.

7. mediate (mē′dē-āt′) v.
The judge was asked to **mediate** the disagreement over property lines between the two parties.

__c__ **Mediate** means
a. incite a riot.
b. evict after judgment.
c. negotiate.
d. interrupt.

8. mutual (myōō′chōō-əl) adj.
Rob's family has a **mutual** understanding that in case of an evacuation, everyone is to make the five-hour drive to the west and meet at the family farm.

__a__ **Mutual** means
a. relating to things in common.
b. uncommon.
c. dull.
d. exciting.

9. proxy (prŏk′sē) n.
Every quarter you will be asked to mail in a vote by **proxy** for board members overseeing your stock.

__c__ **Proxy** means
a. someone disciplined after great consideration.
b. serious expression after great consideration.
c. alternate.
d. well-researched.

10. surrogate (sûr′ə-gĭt) n.
When a woman cannot successfully carry a child to full term, she may choose a **surrogate**—a woman who agrees to be implanted with a fertilized egg and give birth; however, the baby will be raised by someone other than the birth mother.

__b__ **Surrogate** means
a. relative.
b. substitute.
c. grandmother.
d. brothers or sisters.

EXERCISE 2 Word Sorts

Synonyms

Match the word to the synonyms or definitions that follow each blank.

1. bureaucracy organization; administration; red tape
2. mediate arbitrate; intercede; intervene
3. proxy substitute; alternative; stand-in
4. mutual joint; shared; common
5. locus central location; hub

Antonyms

Select the letter of the word(s) with the opposite meaning.

__a__ **6.** ascertain
a. guess b. surround c. determine d. confirm

__b__ **7.** incompetent
a. careless b. talented c. reckless d. shy

__c__ **8.** convey
a. explain b. articulate c. garble d. communicate

__d__ **9.** advocate
a. supporter b. backer c. sponsor d. opponent

d **10.** surrogate

a. replacement
b. stand-in
c. proxy
d. actual participant

EXERCISE 3 Fill in the Blank

Use context clues to determine the word that best completes each sentence.

1. To convey their feelings, some men are more comfortable building things rather than composing love letters or romantic poems.

2. After the bridge stress test failed, the main engineer was relieved of his duties because the owners felt he was incompetent, and Mr. Seaborn was then assigned to supervise for the duration of the project.

3. The Big Brother/Big Sister program does not provide surrogate(s) to act as substitutes for a parent; instead, the volunteers act as role models who help complement the family's needs.

4. Faculty advisors are often the advocate(s) for college students, especially if they are the first generation in their family to continue their education beyond high school.

5. The result of bureaucracy is often a great deal of paperwork sent to many offices within an organization—none of which communicate with each other.

6. To avoid another baseball strike, negotiators were brought in to mediate the disagreement between the owners and the players.

7. The intensity of the eye contact across the room indicated a mutual attraction and prompted Nate to walk over and introduce himself to the woman standing by the window.

8. To ascertain how to begin a drawing in the AutoCad program, a designer first needs to determine what scale would best fit on each sheet.

9. The locus of the city during the unexpected emergency became city hall, where officials could monitor the evacuation as well as the status of people being admitted to the shelters.

10. Any document signed by proxy, that is, when a person is not attending the shareholders' meeting and thus is represented by someone else, must be filed with the Securities and Exchange Commission of the United States.

EXERCISE 4 Application

Using context clues, insert the vocabulary word in the appropriate blank. A part-of-speech clue is given for each vocabulary word.

Nature often provides insight into behavioral science that helps us understand human motivation as well. For example, to **(1)** (v.) ascertain the importance of role models and **(2)** (n.) advocate(s) to support younger members of society, consider an incident that occurred between 1992 and 1997 in Pilanesburg, South Africa. There, young, orphaned male elephants were introduced to the **(3)** (n.) locus of a game reserve, but they proved to be extremely aggressive, attacking and killing more than 40 white rhinos. Soon thereafter, six older male elephants were brought in, and each became a natural **(4)** (n.) proxy, a stand-in parent, for the younger elephants. The presence of the older males provided **(5)** (adj.) mutual calming influences in the younger elephants and their presence helped more than any human attempts to **(6)** (v.) mediate the differences and fix the situation. Eventually, the killing and aggressive behavior of the young elephants diminished.

Another example began as a 1957 experiment of Harry Harlow, his wife, and their associates who explored the effects of **(7)** (n.) surrogates, or artificial mothers, on infant monkeys. During their observations, they found that the young monkeys preferred warmth, softness, and rocking—even if some of these features were from a wire substitute. Although many new parents fear they will be **(8)** (adj.) incompetent, this is comforting information because giving a baby warmth, softness, and rocking motion are things all parents can begin to do to **(9)** (v.) convey their love.

Sometimes humans form organizations with a variety of departments in a web of **(10)** (n.) bureaucracy________, but solutions seem elusive. Perhaps we need to look at the animal kingdom for a simpler answer.

Stop and Think

KIM

Choose any five words and in the boxes below, fill in the key word, information about the word, and then a picture you think represents the word to help you connect to a mental image. (Answers will vary.)

Key Word	Information About the Word	Image

Go to **http://www.patientadvocate.org/** and explore the site. On your own paper, explain whether or not you feel this is a helpful service for patients and their families. Then explain your answer. (Answers will vary.)

CHAPTER

6

Vocabulary in Biology

Get Ready to Read About Biology

Since 60 percent of high school students take biology, it is a course they often select in college to fulfill the lab science requirement for their curriculum. Topics in a college biology textbook range from the life of a cell to ecology and the earth's diverse ecosystem. The selection you are going to read is a case study on blood doping and its adverse effects on an athlete's heart. Before you read, consider what you already know about the following word parts. The meanings of some have been provided. Recall what you learned in Chapter 1 and fill in the blanks for the others.

1. The prefix *ex-* means out, from, away.
2. The prefix *pre-* means before.
3. The suffix *-ize* means make, cause to become and indicates a verb.

aggrandize	crude	expulsion	marrow	premier
arcane	doping	grueling	molecule	segment

CASE STUDY: AN UNFAIR ADVANTAGE

On a sunny July morning in 1998, the members of the Festina bicycle racing team, the top-rated team in the world, sat in a French café. Nearby, dozens of professional bicyclists made their final preparations for the impending start of the day's **segment** of the **grueling** Tour de France race. The

Festina riders, however, would not be joining the race. Hours earlier, the entire team had been expelled from the Tour de France for the offense of blood **doping.**

The dramatic **expulsion** of top athletes from the world's **premier** bicycle race focused attention on the **arcane** practice of blood doping. By using blood-doping techniques, some athletes try to gain the competitive edge. But what is blood doping, and how does it **aggrandize** athletic performance?

Blood doping increases a person's physical endurance by increasing the capacity of the blood to carry oxygen. One **crude** method for accomplishing this goal is to simply inject extra red blood cells into the bloodstream. Red blood cells transport oxygen to the body's tissues, so simply adding more of them is a straightforward way of increasing the amount of oxygen that reaches the tissues. In recent years, however, blood-doping athletes have increasingly turned to injections of erythropoietin (EPO) as a more effective approach to increase blood oxygen.

EPO is a protein **molecule** that is present in a normal human body, where it functions as a chemical messenger that stimulates bone **marrow** to produce more red blood cells. Under normal circumstances, the body produces just enough EPO to ensure that red blood cells are replaced as they age and die. An injection of extra EPO, however, can stimulate the production of a huge number of extra red blood cells. The extra cells greatly increase the oxygen-carrying capacity of the blood. Unfortunately, the excess blood cells also thicken the blood and make it harder to move through blood vessels, so those who inject EPO suffer increased risk of heart failure.

—Adapted from Audersirk, Audersirk, and Byers, *Life on Earth*, 3rd ed. p. 95 Prentice Hall. Reprinted with permission.

VISUAL VOCABULARY

Athletes train in b__________ ways to be ready for a game.

a. crude
b. grueling

Courtesy of Microsoft.

EXERCISE 1 Context Clues

Refer to the previous passage and use context clues from the sentences below to determine the definition of each of the following words in **bold** print. Do not consult a dictionary.

1. aggrandize (ə-grăn′dīz′) v.
To **aggrandize** their image in the community, one family bought an expensive house, but then they could not afford any furniture.

__a__ **Aggrandize** means
a. increase. b. decrease. c. delete. d. discover.

2. arcane (är-kān′) adj.
"The Society of Seven," explained an upperclassman to some incoming freshmen, "is a secret organization with **arcane** practices known only to its selective and unpublished list of members."

__c__ **Arcane** means
a. outstanding. c. mysterious.
b. commonplace. d. well-known.

3. crude (kro͞od) adj.
Lost in the woods with no means of defense, Adam constructed a **crude** weapon and tool by lashing a sturdy limb to a sharp rock.

__b__ **Crude** means
a. polished. b. primitive. c. civil. d. refined.

4. doping (dō′pĭng) n.
Athletes who are pressured to perform at high levels each year may resort to **doping** with anabolic steroids, a practice that will also endanger their lives.

__d__ **Doping** means
a. exercising.
b. rinsing.
c. designing a program with no specific outcome in mind.
d. use of a drug or blood product to improve athletic performance.

5. expulsion (ĭk-spŭl′shən) n.
Umpires used the threat of **expulsion** from the stadium as an attempt to control the unruly fans.

__a__ **Expulsion** means
a. banishing. b. welcoming. c. agreeing. d. accepting.

6. grueling (gro͞o′ə-lĭng) adj.
After several **grueling** nights of studying, reading, writing, and memorizing, Naomi decided to take a few hours off from her hard work and enjoy time with her friends.

__c__ **Grueling** means
a. acceptable. b. soothing. c. agonizing. d. easy.

7. marrow (măr′ō) n.
For Ben, the **marrow** of life involved doing valuable work that connected him in a compassionate way with others who needed his help.

__a__ **Marrow** means
a. innermost part.
b. edge.
c. lack.
d. nothingness.

8. molecule (mŏl′ĭ-kyo͞ol′) n.
A sensitive man, Matt respected all of life right down to its simplest **molecule**.

__d__ **Molecule** means
a. guess. b. view. c. total. d. tiny particle.

9. premier (prĭ-mîr′) adj.
The gallery was famous for exhibiting only the work of **premier** artists, so it was almost impossible for an unknown to be allowed a showing.

__d__ **Premier** means
a. inferior. b. working. c. unpopular. d. leading.

10. segment (sĕg′mənt) n.
Although the first part of the film starts slowly, the last **segment** is nonstop excitement.

__b__ **Segment** means
a. total. b. portion. c. loss. d. composite.

EXERCISE 2 WORD SORTS

Synonyms

Match the word to the synonyms or definitions that follow each blank.

1. __doping__ use of a drug or blood product to augment athletic performance
2. __segment__ portion; part; section

3. molecule particle; iota; fragment

4. marrow essence; gist; fatty network of connective tissue that fills the cavities of the bones

5. expulsion exclusion; exile; deportment

Antonyms

Select the letter of the word(s) with the opposite meaning.

c 6. arcane
a. secret b. hidden c. obvious d. cryptic

c 7. premier
a. leading b. chief c. minor d. major

a 8. grueling
a. easy b. difficult c. harsh d. severe

c 9. crude
a. primitive b. unrefined c. polished d. abrupt

a 10. aggrandize
a. diminish b. increase c. enhance d. reward

EXERCISE 3 Fill in the Blank

Use context clues to determine the word that best completes each sentence.

1. If a salamander accidentally loses a segment of its tail, it has the ability to regenerate another.

2. The dwellings of the colonists who traveled to North America to establish Jamestown were crude, lacking the special features of the homes many of them had left behind in England.

3. Beneath the Sir Christopher Wren Building on the campus of the College of William and Mary is an arcane burial crypt, but no one is quite sure who is buried there.

4. When the opposing team finished the meet with almost super-human times, many speculated the swimmers had used doping to increase the oxygen levels in their blood.

5. "Four exams in two days," complained Ruth Ann, "have proved to be my most grueling college experience yet."

6. The grand opening of the new performing arts center revealed that it was the premier ______ architectural structure in the city.

7. To aggrandize ______ himself in the eyes of the college, the new president projected a large photograph of himself surrounded by young children, as an old friend read a list of his accomplishments and awards.

8. Prior to the beginning of the play, audience members were cautioned about using proper behavior; otherwise, the result would be their expulsion ______ from the theater, and no refund would be granted.

9. Following surgery and chemotherapy, Sandy debated with her insurance company over the merits of a bone marrow ______ transplant, which she felt would increase her chances of survival.

10. According to the American Heart Association, trans fats are fats containing a type of fatty acid molecule ______ that has a trans double bond; often used in the cooking oil for french fries, they affect the body differently from other fats found in nature.

Source: Daily Press, 6/20/06, A1

EXERCISE 4 APPLICATION

Using context clues, insert the vocabulary word in the appropriate blank. A part-of-speech clue is given for each vocabulary word.

American students often complain about the stress they feel over SATs and the intense pressure they feel when filling out college applications. In China, however, the **(1)** (n.) segment ______ of students who hope to be admitted to college must prepare for years for one **(2)** (adj.) grueling ______ test that will determine their fate.

What makes the process so rigorous? The reason is that in China, there are over 8 million high school students competing for only 2 million positions, and the decision to admit a student is based on a three-digit test score. To be accepted, there is no **(3)** (adj.) arcane ______ or secret formula of mental **(4)** (n.) doping ______, no special treatment for the country's **(5)** (adj.) premier ______ family members, no opportunity to

(6) (v.) aggrandize ______ their abilities through letters of recommendation or eloquent essays. Instead, the students must know English, math, history, and science. And they must know a wide range of information from the simplest **(7)** (n.) molecule ______ to the most complex concepts.

To many the process seems cruel—a **(8)** (adj.) crude ______, primitive way to sift through millions of applications. As a result of their studying, many students develop stress-related health problems. To them, the idea of not being admitted to a college is akin to **(9)** (n.) expulsion ______ from society. It is as if the **(10)** (n.) marrow ______ of their existence has been destroyed. Likewise, many parents feel like failures if their children are disappointed.

The solution in China has been to create substantive private colleges. It is hoped that providing more opportunities will ease the burden for everyone.

Stop and Think

Pyramid Word Card

Select a word from the chapter and complete the pyramid below with the appropriate information. (Answers will vary, but an example is given.)

1. Write the vocabulary word.
2. List three synonyms (one-word definitions).
3. List the word parts and definitions (if available).
4. List antonyms (opposites) of the word.
5. Write a sentence using the word.

aggrandize

enhance, improve, enlarge

from the Latin *grandire,* which means large

diminish, reduce, belittle, deflate, humble, lower, disgrace

James told everyone about his volunteer work in order to aggrandize himself.

Complete the following sentences. (Answers will vary.)

1. The most frustrating thing about bureaucracy is the ________________.
2. One of the most arcane things I have ever read about is ________________.
3. If I were a member of the premier family of our country, I would make sure to ________________.
4. The most grueling experience I have ever had was when I ________________.
5. When I think of athletes using blood doping or other means to enhance their performance, I ________________.

CHAPTER 7

Vocabulary in Science Issues

Get Ready to Read About Science Issues

College is a time for researching current issues—many of which are more comprehensible with a background in science. In this selection, you will read about a community health concern, which is the effects of tick bites and their possible subsequent side effects. Before you read, consider what you already know about the following word parts. The meanings of some have been provided. Recall what you learned in Chapter 1 and fill in the blanks for the others.

1. The prefix *con-* means with, together.
2. The prefix *in-* means in, inside.
3. The suffix *-an* means belonging to.
4. The suffix *-ate* means make, cause to become and usually indicates a verb.
5. The suffix *-or* means *something or one who does* and usually indicates a noun.

arsenal	constrict	host	inhibitor	mammalian
coagulate	counter	ingest	malady	platelet

TICK SALIVA AND LYME DISEASE

When a tick finds a **mammalian host** and begins to chew through its skin to reach some nourishing blood, the host's body responds rapidly. The blood in the wound begins to **coagulate** to seal the rupture, blood components known as **platelets** collect around the wound to plug the hole, and nearby blood vessels **constrict** to reduce blood loss. Special cells and chemical agents move to the wound to inflame it and destroy any invading bacteria.

The tick's saliva **counters** all of these defensive efforts. As the tick chews toward a blood vessel, its saliva dribbles into the wound, carrying a chemical mixture that includes painkillers to prevent the host from noticing the attack, anti-coagulants that prevent blood clots, platelet **inhibitors** that prevent the platelets from clumping, vasodilators that prevent blood vessels from constricting, anti-inflammatories that dampen inflammation of the wound, and even substances that interfere with chemical signaling among the cells from the host's defense system. This salivary **arsenal** is all part of the tick's effort to remain aboard its host and to keep the blood flowing. Unfortunately for the host, the tick's chemical weaponry also creates conditions for the entry of microscopic parasites that can cause disease.

For many of these disease-causing microorganisms, the tick itself is the vehicle for transportation from victim to victim. For example, the bacterium *Borrelia burgdorferi* lives in the bodies of mice, deer, and humans. If a deer tick takes a meal from an infected mouse or deer, it may **ingest** some *Borrelia* bacteria. The bacteria can survive in the tick's gut and, if the tick later latches onto a human, the bacteria can move from the tick's gut to the human host. An infected human may exhibit a bull's-eye-shaped rash, fever, and flu-like symptoms. This **malady,** known as Lyme disease, can usually be treated effectively with antibiotics but, if undiagnosed or untreated, it can cause nerve damage and chronic arthritis.

The incidence of Lyme disease has been increasing in recent years, inspiring development of a vaccine against it. Like all vaccines, the Lyme disease vaccine takes advantage of the body's own mechanisms for combating disease.

—Audersirk, Audersirk, and Byers, *Life on Earth*, 3rd ed. p. 417. Prentice Hall. Reprinted with permission.

VISUAL VOCABULARY

When exploring in the woods, be sure to have a(n) a_______ of medications for first aid and the treatment of insect bites.

a. arsenal
b. malady

George Pongratz

EXERCISE 1 Context Clues

Refer to the previous passage and use context clues from the sentences below to determine the definition of each of the following words in **bold** print. Do not consult a dictionary.

1. arsenal (är′sə-nəl) n.
To prepare for her final exams, Chrystal used an **arsenal** of study strategies such as memory cards, concept maps, graphic organizers, summaries, and taped lectures.

__b__ **Arsenal** means
a. accident. b. storehouse. c. cooperation. d. division.

2. coagulate (kō-ăg′yə-lāt) v.
When Samantha left the gravy on the table too long, it began to **coagulate** and soon looked like brown Jell-o.

__c__ **Coagulate** means
a. encompass. b. escape. c. clot. d. flow.

3. constrict (kən-strĭkt′) v.
Instead of using a scale to determine if he has gained weight, Joe goes on a diet when his belt **constricts** his waistline.

__a__ **Constrict** means
a. squeeze. b. spear. c. expand. d. inflate.

4. counter (koun′tər) v.
When shopping for a new car, Ben negotiated with the salesman, who made an offer; then Ben **countered** his offer in an effort to pay a lower price.

__a__ **Counter** means
a. assert in contrast.
b. agree in harmony.
c. consider seriously.
d. increase.

5. host (hōst) n.
Mistletoe, though charming in the winter, is a partial parasite that attaches to a **host** such as a wide range of trees, but it also produces evergreen leaves that provide a means of photosynthesis for survival as well.

__d__ **Host** means
a. organism that lives in another.
b. damage done by accident.
c. entertainment.
d. living organism on which another organism lives.

6. ingest (ĭn-jĕst′) v.
In case a child **ingests** a substance you suspect is toxic, contact the local poison control organization immediately.

__c__ **Ingest** means
a. require.
b. avoid.
c. take in for digestion.
d. expel.

7. inhibitor (ĭn-hĭb′ĭ-tər) n.
Because it is used to treat hypertension and congestive heart failure, some people take an ACE **inhibitor,** a medication that prevents the Angiotension Converting Enzyme.

__d__ **Inhibitor** means
a. something that encourages.
b. something that predicts.
c. something that promotes.
d. something that prevents.

8. malady (măl′ə-dē) n.
A childhood **malady** such as measles or mumps has not posed a threat in most developed nations because of the availability of vaccines; however, in many third world countries, these illnesses abound in poor areas.

__a__ **Malady** means
a. illness seen in animals and humans.
b. memory.
c. benefit.
d. similarity.

9. mammalian (mă-mā′lē-ən) adj.
The blue whale has **mammalian** traits such as mammary glands for feeding its young, dentition, and even hair-like fibers on its body.

__d__ **Mammalian** means
a. scale-bearing.
b. cold-blooded.
c. characterized by warm-blooded invertebrates.
d. characterized by warm-blooded higher vertebrates.

10. platelet (plāt′lĭt) n.
Some blood drives are for blood plasma if there is a need to enhance the **platelets** of a patient.

__a__ **Platelet** means
a. cytoplasmic body found in blood that promotes clotting.
b. small surgical utensil.
c. hospital policy.
d. bacteria-carrying substance.

EXERCISE 2 Word Sorts

Synonyms

Match the word to the synonyms or definitions that follow each blank.

1. platelet ______ a minute, irregularly shaped, disklike cytoplasmic body found in blood plasma that promotes blood clotting and has no definite nucleus, no DNA, and no hemoglobin
2. mammalian ______ any of various warm-blooded vertebrate animals of the class Mammalia, including humans, characterized by a covering of hair on the skin and, in the female, milk-producing mammary glands for nourishing the young
3. coagulate ______ clot; coalesce; gelatinize
4. host ______ animal or plant on which another lives
5. arsenal ______ storage place; vault; storehouse

Antonyms

Select the letter of the word(s) with the opposite meaning.

b ___ **6.** counter
a. cross b. accept c. circumvent d. hinder

a ___ **7.** malady
a. health b. sickness c. illness d. entertainment

c ___ **8.** inhibitor
a. something that thwarts c. promoter
b. prevention d. successor

b ___ **9.** ingest
a. consume b. discharge c. soak up d. digest

c ___ **10.** constrict
a. squeeze b. tighten c. expand d. shrink

EXERCISE 3 Fill in the Blank

Use context clues to determine the word that best completes each sentence.

1. One inhibitor ______ to learning is constant criticism.
2. To prevent the possibility of hemorrhaging during surgery, prospective patients are cautioned to stop taking aspirin or vitamin E, because the

blood will not coagulate as well since both substances are blood thinners.

3. Will's medicine chest was an arsenal of cold medications, so if any of his neighbors suddenly needed a decongestant or nasal spray in the middle of the night, they would call him.

4. During the presidential debate, one candidate calmly counter(ed) all criticisms with confident humor and was perceived as the more assertive and likeable of the two.

5. Remoras, or sucker fish, often attach to a host such as sharks, rays, whales and turtles.

6. Columbian boas fare well in captivity and become docile; instead of constrict(ing) and endangering their owners, they often become devoted and faithful pets.

7. Hyperthyroidism, a disease in which the thyroid gland is overly active, has three treatments: surgery; radioiodine; and the administration of thyrostatics, or drugs that act as inhibitor(s) of thyroid hormones.

8. Mammalian traits, such as being warm-blooded and having a four-chambered heart, are shared by more than 5,500 species, including humans.

9. Some researchers believe that arthritis is one malady that can be the result of a tick bite.

10. To earn extra money while in college, Josh gave blood from which his platelet(s) were extracted and separated and later used for cancer patients.

EXERCISE 4 Application

Using context clues, insert the vocabulary word in the appropriate blank. A part-of-speech clue is given for each vocabulary word.

Doctors use the scientific method when trying to determine the cause of someone's symptoms—especially when they are not sure of the exact source. For example, the test for blood **(1)** (n.) platelet count, also known as a thrombocyte count, may be ordered in conjunction with a CBC, complete blood count, to diagnose a **(2)** (n.) malady such as a bleeding disorder or a bone marrow disease.

The thrombocytes, or platelets, are tiny fragments in **(3)** (adj.) mammalian________ cells made in the bone marrow that circulate in the blood. Because they are very sticky, they are the first components to be activated when there is an injury, and they promote **(4)** (n.) coagulation________, or clotting. Thus, they are **(5)** (n.) inhibitor(s)________ of conditions that might cause hemorrhaging, or "bleeding out" of a patient.

A test for a platelet count is ordered in a variety of situations. One is when a bacteria is **(6)** (v.) ingest(ed)________ through contaminated food causing salmonella. Another is in the contraction of bacteria from a flea that has bitten a contaminated rat. Thus, that bacteria uses the human blood as its **(7)** (n.) host________ for survival. The result, in this case, would be the disease known as the Bubonic Plague.

To **(8)** (v.) counter________ such diseases, the doctor will prescribe an **(9)** (n.) arsenal________ of additional tests and then antibiotics. Sometimes, patients do not realize the necessity of medical assessments for a proper diagnosis. They want instant relief. Instead of viewing the extensive testing as something that **(10)** (v.) constrict(s)________ our lives, we should view it as a channel to freedom from pain.

—Adapted from http://www.labtestsonline.org/understanding/analytes/cbc/sample.html

Stop and Think

Complete the Frayer model for the word *counter*.

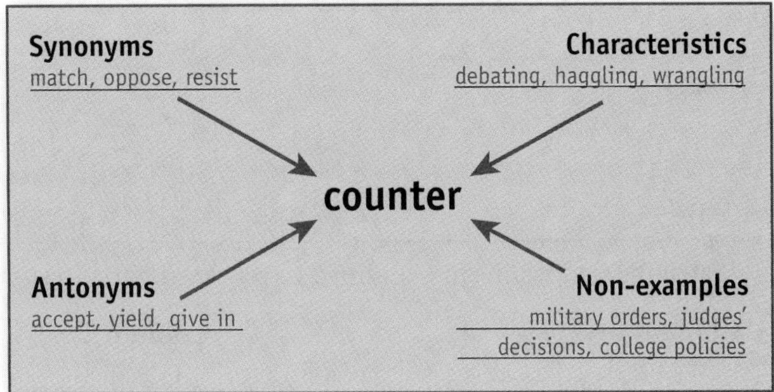

Connect one of the following words to the comic below, and then explain your reason. (arsenal, constrict, inhibitor) (Answers will vary.)

Source: Bruce Tinsley *Daily Press*, June 19, 2006/King Features Syndicate

Review Test
Chapters 3–7

1 Word Parts

Match the definitions in Column 2 to the word parts in Column 1.

Column 1	Column 2
h **1.** sub-	a. time, order
g **2.** -tion	b. place
a **3.** chron	c. throw
c **4.** ject	d. study, science of
d **5.** -ology	e. cause to become, make
i **6.** voc	f. from, away
b **7.** loc	g. action, process
j **8.** pre-	h. under, below
e **9.** -ize	i. call
f **10.** ex-	j. before

2 Fill in the Blank

Use context clues to determine the best word from the box to complete each sentence.

alienation	causation	convey	expulsion	incompetent
ameliorate	comply	doping	host	ingest

1. After two drug tests revealed abnormally high levels of synthetic testosterone, the athlete was accused of chemical doping ________, which was an infraction that would eliminate him from the event.

2. Tito's constant smile convey(ed) ________ the joy he felt about his new job.

3. When he first moved to the area, Victor felt a sense of isolation and alienation ________; however, after a few visits to the International Club, he felt like a part of the group.

4. When Mark accidentally ingest(ed) ________ the toxin, his lab partner immediately notified the Poison Control Center to determine the treatment.

5. Lori's career plans changed suddenly when she decided she wanted to ameliorate ________ human suffering rather than amass a fortune at the expense of the powerless.

6. The college fraternity faced expulsion ________ from campus when they were found guilty of hazing that was dangerous enough to put three of their pledges in the hospital.

7. In spite of excellent training, the new intern suddenly felt incompetent ________ as she began her field experience in teaching.

8. The 1979 film *Alien* is a frightening story about organisms from another planet that use humans as host(s) ________ for the incubation of their eggs.

9. When the experimental MagLev, a magnetic monorail at Old Dominion University, failed in the initial testing, engineers scrambled to determine the causation ________ of the problem.

10. To rent the house, Bentley had to sign a contract and agree to comply ________ with the rules set by the landlord.

2

3 Book Connection

Use context clues to determine the best word from the box to complete each sentence. A part of speech clue is provided for each vocabulary word.

aggrandize	arcane	degradation	impasse	remission
aggression	ascertain	exacerbation	mutual	surrogate

THE KITE RUNNER

Opening in pre-Taliban Afghanistan, *The Kite Runner* by Khaled Hossieni is the story of friendship and betrayal, shame and redemption. The protagonist, Amir, has a happy youth in Kabul with Baba, his father, Ali, his father's servant, and Hassan, his best friend and servant. It is a charmed life until Amir witnesses an act of **(1)** (n.) aggression against Hassan—an act that causes the humiliation and emotional **(2)** (n.) degradation of his friend. It is also an event that Amir does not stop. As a result of his cowardice, Amir alienates his friend, who is wise beyond his years and continues to try to make Amir's life easier. However, when their friendship reaches an **(3)** (n.) impasse, Hassan and his father Ali leave the household out of a need to save their own honor. The separation creates a hole in the hearts of Amir and his father, who eventually flee to the United States when Taliban makes life dangerously impossible.

Amir's father develops a great love for America, but his stay is short-lived after he is diagnosed with cancer. Baba refuses treatment since **(4)** (n.) remission is not guaranteed, only that the **(5)** (n.) exacerbation of his pain will be slower. At the same time, Amir meets Saroya, also from Afghanistan, and their friendship develops into a **(6)** (adj.) mutual love. They marry with Baba's blessings. Despite their goodness, both are haunted by past ghosts and long for forgiveness.

That chance for forgiveness comes in the unlikely form of a summons back to Afghanistan. Once there, Amir **(7)** (v.) ascertain(s) that Rahim Khan, a man who was also like a **(8)** (n.) surrogate to Amir, is dying, and there is little time to **(9)** (v.) aggrandize himself in the eyes of this man who had been an inspiration when he reveals a new secret and makes a request. There is no **(10)** (adj.) arcane, secret formula for redemption. Instead, Rahim Khan offers Amir a "way to be good again." This time, however, it means facing the ghosts of the past and risking his own life to save another.

4 Visual Connection

Write a caption for this picture using two of the words from the box. (Answers will vary.)

arsenal	grueling	marrow	modality	segment
coagulate	inhibitor	mediate	platelet	subside

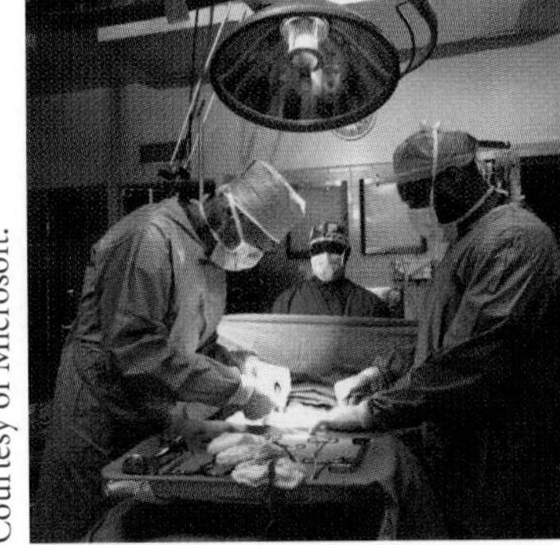

Courtesy of Microsoft.

____

____

____

____

____

____

5 Analogies

Choose the word that best completes the analogy.

1. weakness : strength :: passivity : c
   a. duration b. bureaucracy c. assertiveness

2. addition : subtraction :: invisible : b______________
   a. incompetent   b. discernible   c. subjective

3. short : height :: brief : a______________
   a. duration   b. expulsion   c. alienation

4. impartial : prejudiced :: objective : a______________
   a. subjective   b. mutual   c. discernible

5. waiting : registration :: red tape : c______________
   a. malady   b. assertiveness   c. bureaucracy

6. stimulating : boring :: sophistication : c______________
   a. incompetent   b. arcane   c. crude

7. flower : petal :: water : a______________
   a. molecule   b. aggression   c. degradation

8. stretch : expand :: squeeze : b______________
   a. ascertain   b. constrict   c. subside

9. subpoena : issue :: argument : c______________
   a. constrict   b. demean   c. counter

10. cold-blooded : warm-blooded :: reptilian : a______________
    a. mammalian   b. snake   c. turtle

UNIT 3 Vocabulary in Social Sciences

CHAPTER

8

Vocabulary in Psychology

Get Ready to Read About Psychology

Psychology is the study of mental processes and behavior. The word *psychology* comes from the root word *psych*, which means *mind*, and the suffix *–ology*, which means *study of*. As you read issues about psychology, you will make connections to your own experiences, and you will grow to understand yourself and others better so you can develop *autonomy*—that is, independence.

Before you read, consider what you already know about the following word parts. The meanings of some have been provided. Recall what you learned in Chapter 1 and fill in the blanks for the others.

1. The prefix *ex-* means from, away.
2. The prefix *per-* means through.
3. The root *cog* means *know*.
4. The suffix *-ate* means cause to become, make and usually indicates a verb.

adaptive	cognition	differentiate	impulsive	persistence
coercive	defiance	exert	overindulge	resort

CHILD-REARING STYLES

Child-rearing styles are combinations of parenting behaviors that occur over a wide range of situations, creating an enduring child-rearing climate. In a landmark series of studies, Diana Baumrind gathered information on child rearing by watching parents interact with their preschoolers. Her findings, and those of others who have extended her work, reveal three features that consistently **differentiate** an authoritative style from less effective styles: (1) acceptance and involvement, (2) control, and (3) autonomy granting (Gray & Steinberg, 1999; Hart, Newell, & Olson, 2002).

Authoritative Child Rearing

The authoritative style—the most successful approach to child rearing—involves high acceptance and involvement, **adaptive** control techniques, and appropriate autonomy granting. Authoritative parents are warm, attentive, and sensitive to their child's needs. They establish an enjoyable, emotionally fulfilling parent-child relationship that draws the child into close connection. At the same time, authoritative parents exercise firm, reasonable control; they insist on mature behavior and give reasons for their expectations. Finally, authoritative parents engage in gradual, appropriate autonomy granting, allowing the child to make decisions in areas where he is ready to make choices (Kuczynski & Lollis, 2002; Russell, Mize, & Bisaker).

Throughout childhood and adolescence, authoritative parenting is linked to many aspects of competence. These include an upbeat mood, self-control, task **persistence,** cooperativeness, high self-esteem, social and moral maturity, and favorable school performance (Baumrind & Black, 1967; Herman et al., 1997; Luster & McAdoo, 1996; Steinberg, Darling, & Fletcher, 1995).

Authoritarian Child Rearing

Parents who use an authoritarian style are low in acceptance and involvement, high in **coercive** control, and low in autonomy granting. Authoritarian parents appear cold and rejecting; they frequently degrade their child by putting her down. To **exert** control, they yell, command, and criticize. "Do it because I said so!" is the attitude of these parents. If the child disobeys, authoritarian parents **resort** to force and punishment. In addition, they make decisions for their child and expect the child to accept their word in an unquestioning manner. If the child does not, authoritarian parents resort to force and punishment.

Children of authoritarian parents are anxious and unhappy. When interacting with peers, they tend to react with hostility when frustrated. Boys especially show high rates of anger and **defiance.** Girls are dependent, lacking in exploration, and overwhelmed by challenging tasks (Baumrind, 1971; Hart et al., 2002; Nix et al., 1999).

Permissive Child Rearing

The permissive style of child rearing is warm and accepting. But rather than being involved, such parents are **overindulging** or inattentive. Permissive parents engage in little control of their child's behavior. And instead of gradually granting autonomy, they allow children to make many of their own decisions at an age when they are not yet capable of doing so. Their children can eat meals and go to bed when they feel like it and watch as much television as they want. They do not have to learn good manners or do any household chores. Although some permissive parents truly believe that this approach is best, many others lack confidence in their ability to influence their child's behavior.

Children of permissive parents are **impulsive,** disobedient, and rebellious. They are also overly demanding and dependent on adults, and they show less persistence on tasks than children whose parents exert more control. The link between permissive parenting and dependent, nonachieving behavior is especially strong for boys (Barber & Olsen, 1997; Baumrind, 1971).

Uninvolved Parenting

The uninvolved style combines low acceptance and involvement with little control and general indifference to autonomy granting. Often these parents are emotionally detached and depressed and so overwhelmed by life stress that they have little time and energy for children (Maccoby & Martin, 1983). At its extreme, uninvolved parenting is a form of child maltreatment called neglect. Especially when it begins early, it disrupts virtually all aspects of development, including attachment, **cognition,** and emotional and social skills.

—Berk, *Development Through the Lifespan*, 3rd ed., pp. 265–66.
Longman Publishers. Reprinted with permission.

VISUAL VOCABULARY

Good parents a__________ time and energy to provide a good home life for their children.

a. exert
b. differentiate

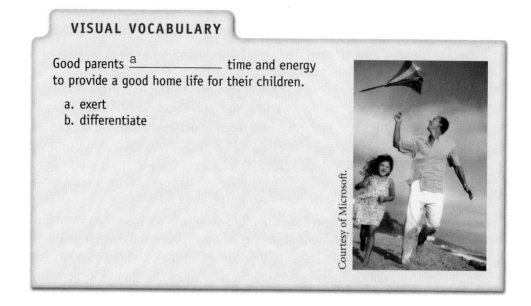

Courtesy of Microsoft.

EXERCISE 1 Context Clues

Refer to the previous passage and use context clues from the sentences below to determine the definition of each of the following words in **bold** print. Do not consult a dictionary.

1. adaptive (ə-dăp′tĭv) adj.
Animals such as the chameleon are so **adaptive** to their environment that they are able to change colors to blend in with their surroundings.

__b__ **Adaptive** means
a. awkward.
b. capable of fitting in.
c. capable of showing sensitivity to others' feelings.
d. easy.

2. coercive (kō-ûr′sĭv) adj.
Coercive measures such as yelling and verbal abuse are less effective in shaping behavior than less forceful techniques.

__c__ **Coercive** means
a. voluntary. b. excitable. c. overbearing. d. yielding.

3. cognition (kŏg-nĭsh′ən) n.
According to psychologists, even unborn babies are capable of some form of **cognition** before birth because some learn to suck their thumbs *in utero*, and they recognize voices immediately after delivery.

__a__ **Cognition** means
a. awareness. b. ignorance. c. acceptance. d. allegiance.

4. defiance (dĭ-fī′əns) n.
Although he was an acclaimed military leader in World War II, General Douglas McArthur was relieved of his command during the Korean War because of his acts of **defiance** against President Harry Truman's policies.

__d__ **Defiance** means
a. authority. b. surrender. c. obedience. d. disagreement.

5. differentiate (dĭf′ə-rĕn′shē-āt′) v.
The twins were not identical, but their physical traits were so similar that it was almost impossible to **differentiate** between the two.

__d__ **Differentiate** means
a. arrange.
b. mistake.
c. confuse.
d. make distinction.

6. exert (ĭg-zûrt′) v.
As the temperatures began to climb, advisories appeared warning people not to **exert** themselves too much in the heat and to try to stay indoors or in the shade during the hours of 10 A.M. and 2 P.M.

__d__ **Exert** means
a. repel. b. fulfill. c. relieve. d. push.

7. impulsive (ĭm-pŭl′sĭv) adj.
Michael's proposal to Adria was **impulsive**, but in spite of his lack of planning, he beautifully expressed a love that was genuine and true.

__b__ **Impulsive** means
a. cautious.
b. spontaneous.
c. thoughtful.
d. well-planned.

8. overindulge (ō′vər-ĭn-dŭlj′) v.
Usually adults who can legally drink alcohol do not **overindulge** the way young college freshmen binge, and some people use this as an argument to oppose lowering the legal drinking age.

__a__ **Overindulge** means
a. give in to excess.
b. limit.
c. expect.
d. ignore as a strategic plan.

9. persistence (pər-sĭs′təns) n.
To teach his children **persistence,** Marcus allows them to make mistakes but never to give up without having tried many times first.

__d__ **Persistence** means
a. indecision. c. limitation.
b. act of changing. d. act of continuing.

10. resort (to) (rĭ-zôrt′) v.
In an effort to cheer each other up during a rainy week at the beach, Sasha and Ornella began to **resort** to exchanging knock-knock jokes.

__c__ **Resort** *(to)* means
a. give up. b. arrive. c. put in effect. d. ignore.

EXERCISE 2 Word Sorts

Synonyms

Match the word to the synonyms or definitions that follow each blank.

1. overindulge pamper; satisfy; gormandize
2. adaptive capable of or suited to fitting in
3. differentiate distinguish; discern; make distinction
4. exert strain; endeavor; struggle
5. cognition understanding; awareness; intelligence

Antonyms

Select the letter of the word(s) with the opposite meaning.

__c__ **6.** defiance
a. disobedience c. surrender
b. challenge d. disregard

__c__ **7.** hostility
a. antagonism c. peace
b. animosity d. disagreement

__a__ **8.** persistence
a. stopping c. insistence
b. continuation d. suggestion

__b__ **9.** coercive
a. domineering c. hardworking
b. yielding d. surrounding

b **10.** impulsive
a. careless
b. cautious
c. emotional
d. sensitive

EXERCISE 3 Fill in the Blank

Use context clues to determine the word that best completes each sentence.

1. Most film producers are considered impulsive and temperamental, but Rudd Simmons, who is known for such works as *High Fidelity, Dead Man Walking, The Royal Tenenbaums,* and *Life Aquatic of Steve Zissou*, is a calm, methodical man—not at all the unpredictable personality one might expect.

2. After a tennis lesson and a piano lesson, and in spite of his exhaustion, James had to work a full shift and then exert more energy late in the evening to study for his French test.

3. Ecologists are studying the adaptive nature of reef-building corals, but they currently do not agree on the best method to help them survive.

4. No matter how much dinner they have had, when visiting The Trellis, patrons usually overindulge and order the Death by Chocolate cake.

5. One of the most famous acts of defiance was when Rosa Parks refused to give up her seat on a bus in Montgomery, Alabama.

6. The Intolerable Acts were coercive measures the British tried to enforce in the colonies in the 18th century and resulted in the meeting of the First Continental Congress in 1774.

7. The amygdala is the area of the brain that prompts the body to flee, freeze, or fight in the face of hostility.

8. Although both computers looked alike, Seth was able to differentiate between the two and identify which would be the better buy.

9. As people age, there are a number of things they can do to help prevent their memory and cognition from deteriorating at a rapid rate.

10. Although he was so poor that he lacked running water or a telephone when growing up, Alberto Gonzales was able to transcend his poverty through persistence, hard work, and good fortune to become a member of the President's staff and serve as Attorney General of the United States.

EXERCISE 4 Application

Using context clues, insert the vocabulary word in the appropriate blank. A part-of-speech clue is given for each vocabulary word.

"If only I could take a pill to enhance my memory," moaned Meg as she studied for her exams.

Have you ever said that? Although it seems like a good idea to improve **(1)** (n.) cognition—that ability to think critically, to remember details, and to **(2)** (v.) differentiate between fact and opinion—learning new ideas requires that we **(3)** (v.) exert effort and move through several stages, things that cannot be accomplished with one little pill.

Another thing psychologists know about learning is that **(4)** (n.) persistence pays. The continuous drill, repetition, and connecting of new information to prior knowledge is a way to grow dendrites, those treelike nerve cells that extend when learning occurs. And although it may seem trite, the idea that practice makes perfect is more than just a common saying. It's true. Repetition helps us move information from short-term, or working memory, to long-term memory, in which case we don't have to **(5)** (v.) resort to cramming the night before a test. Instead, becoming **(6)** (adj.) adaptive to a new and efficient way of reviewing information each day can be almost as good as taking a memory pill.

Other tips that promote learning include having the right attitude. Embracing a demeanor of **(7)** (n.) defiance is counterproductive. Many of us know that any **(8)** (adj.) coercive attitude impedes learning—whether we are being forced by teachers, parents, or other outside forces. Instead, we should be ready to cooperate and work toward a goal of learning, so that the process becomes intrinsic. Also, as college students, we have to develop the maturity to avoid **(9)** (adj.) impulsive tendencies. Suddenly deciding to go to the pub with friends to **(10)** (v.) overindulge________ in drinking alcohol when we have finals in the next few days is not conducive to learning.

Stop and Think

Write a caption for this picture using one of the vocabulary words from this chapter.

Susan Pongratz

(Answers will vary.)

Complete the table with other forms of the words from this chapter. You may need to consult a dictionary or **www.dictionary.com** for reference.

Noun	Verb	Adjective
adaptation	adapt	adaptive
coercion	coerce	coercive
defiance	defy	defiant
persistence	persist	persistent

CHAPTER 9 Vocabulary in Sociology

Get Ready to Read About Sociology

Sociology is the study of human behavior within societies. During a course in sociology, you will study about other cultures and how people interact. You will also study about the values, customs, and traditions held by people worldwide.

Before you read, consider what you already know about the following word parts. Recall what you learned in Chapter 1 and fill in the blanks.

1. The root *psych* means *mind*.
2. The suffix *-ate* means *cause to become, make* and usually indicates a *verb*.
3. The suffix *-ic* means *like, related to* and usually indicates an *adjective*.

accommodate	elusive	inherent	myriad	platonic
altruistic	impairment	mundane	neurotic	psychosomatic

WHAT IS LOVE?

Love—as both an emotion and a behavior—is essential for human survival. The family is usually our earliest and most important source of love and emotional support. Babies and children deprived of love have been known to develop a wide variety of problems that sometimes lasts a lifetime; some of these problems include physiological **impairments** and **neurotic** and **psychosomatic** difficulties. In contrast, infants who are loved and cuddled typically gain more weight, cry less, and smile more.

Actress Mae West once said, "I never loved another person the way I loved myself." Although such a statement may seem self-centered, it's actually quite insightful. Social scientists describe self-love as an important basis for self-esteem. Among other things, people who like themselves are more open to criticism and less demanding of others. People who don't like themselves may not be able to return love but may constantly seek love relationships to bolster their own poor self image. But just what is love? What brings people together?

Love is an **elusive** concept. We have all experienced love and feel we know what it is; however, when asked what love is, people give a variety of answers. According to a 9-year-old boy, for example, "Love is like an avalanche where you have to run for your life." What we mean by love depends on whether we are talking about love for family members, friends, or lovers.

Love has many dimensions. It can be romantic, exciting, obsessive, and irrational. It can also be **platonic,** calming, **altruistic,** and sensible. Many researchers feel that love defies a single definition because it varies in degree and intensity and across social contexts. At the very least, three elements are necessary for a love relationship: (1) a willingness to please and **accommodate** the other, even if this involves compromise and sacrifice; (2) an acceptance of the other person's faults and shortcomings; and (3) as much concern about the loved one's welfare as one's own. And, as you will see shortly, people who say they are "in love" emphasize caring, intimacy, and commitment.

In any type of love, caring about the other person is essential. Although love may involve passionate yearning, respect is a more important quality. Respect is **inherent** in all love: "I want the loved person to grow and unfold for his own sake, and in his own ways, and not for the purpose of serving me." If respect and caring are missing, the relationship is not based on love. Instead, it is an unhealthy or possessive dependency that limits the lovers' social, emotional, and intellectual growth.

Love, especially long-term love, has nothing in common with the images of love or frenzied sex that we get from Hollywood, television, and romance novels. Because of these images, many people believe a variety of myths about love. These misconceptions often lead to unrealistic expectations, stereotypes, and disillusionment. In fact, "real" love is closer to what one author called "stirring-the-oatmeal" love. This type of love is neither exciting nor thrilling but is relatively **mundane** and unromantic. It means paying bills, putting out the garbage, scrubbing the toilet bowls, being up all night with a sick baby, and performing **myriad** other "oatmeal" tasks that are not very sexy.

—Adapted from Benokraitis, *Marriages and Families*, 4th ed., pp. 106–07.

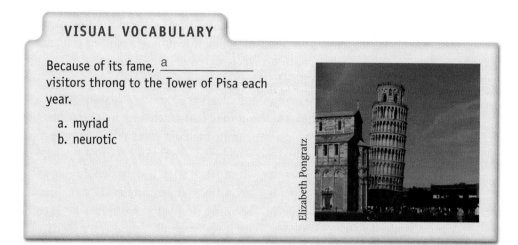

VISUAL VOCABULARY

Because of its fame, <u>a</u> visitors throng to the Tower of Pisa each year.

a. myriad
b. neurotic

Elizabeth Pongratz

EXERCISE 1 Context Clues

Refer to the previous passage and use context clues from the sentences below to determine the definition of each of the following words in **bold** print. Do not consult a dictionary.

1. accommodate (ə-kŏm′ə-dāt′) v.
When making room reservations for the guest speaker, we had to find a room large enough to **accommodate** a crowd of 200.

<u>c</u> **Accommodate** means

a. prevent.
b. confuse.
c. contain; serve.
d. turn away; constrain.

2. altruistic (ăl′trōō-ĭs′tĭk) adj.
In an **altruistic** move, Bill and Melinda Gates are hoping to eliminate 20 diseases by funding immunizations for millions of children worldwide.

<u>a</u> **Altruistic** means

a. generous. b. selfish. c. greedy. d. popular.

3. elusive (ĭ-lōō′sĭv) adj.
Although the secret to success seems **elusive,** most agree you should spend your life in a career you like, and happiness will follow.

__d__ **Elusive** means
a. truthful.
b. actual.
c. easy to grasp.
d. difficult to grasp.

4. impairment (ĭm-pâr′mənt) n.
Because of her visual **impairment,** Tamara traveled to New Jersey to adapt to a guide dog trained to service the blind.

__a__ **Impairment** means
a. disability. b. advantage. c. habit. d. strength.

5. inherent (ĭn-hîr′ənt) adj.
Some people believe that leadership qualities are **inherent,** but other people say that the ability to lead can be learned.

__c__ **Inherent** means
a. learned.
b. unnecessary.
c. basic.
d. acquired.

6. mundane (mŭn-dān′) adj.
After working with numbers all day, the accountant enjoyed **mundane** tasks at home such as weeding the garden, cutting the grass, and trimming the hedges.

__c__ **Mundane** means
a. extraordinary.
b. rare.
c. ordinary.
d. unnecessary.

7. myriad (mĭr′ē-əd) adj.
We studied **myriad** philosophies in our freshman seminar, after which we were assigned a long research paper to present one in depth to the class.

__b__ **Myriad** means
a. few. b. countless. c. sample. d. extension.

8. neurotic (no͞o-rŏt′ĭk) adj.
A **neurotic** man, Sampson is convinced the conspiracy theory is real, and he does not even have a bank account or credit card because he believes the government is trying to track every move he makes.

__b__ **Neurotic** means
a. well-adjusted.
b. maladjusted.
c. fascinating.
d. fundamental.

9. platonic (plə-tŏn′ĭk) adj.
Their friendship began as a **platonic** relationship, but over the years, it grew into true love.

__c__ **Platonic** means
a. convenient. b. physical. c. nonphysical. d. nonspiritual.

10. psychosomatic (sī′kō-sō-măt′ĭk) adj.
Until his doctor could determine the illness, Michael worried that maybe his symptoms were **psychosomatic** with no physical basis.

__b__ **Psychosomatic** means
a. physical.
b. pertaining to the mind.
c. pertaining to the present.
d. pertaining to the past.

EXERCISE 2 Word Sorts

Synonyms

Match the word to the synonyms or definitions that follow each blank.

1. __psychosomatic__ relating to an illness with a mental or emotional origin
2. __neurotic__ relating to excessive anxiety or emotional upset
3. __accommodate__ to shelter; to house; to handle
4. __impairment__ disability; affliction; ailment
5. __platonic__ nonphysical; spiritual; intellectual

Antonyms

Select the letter of the word(s) with the opposite meaning.

__b__ **6.** elusive
a. intangible
b. within reach
c. suggestive
d. praised

__c__ **7.** altruistic
a. unselfish
b. benevolent
c. greedy
d. silent

__a__ **8.** inherent
a. acquired
b. fundamental
c. inborn
d. fragmented

__a__ **9.** mundane
a. extraordinary
b. commonplace
c. ordinary
d. excessive

d **10.** myriad
a. a great number
b. infinity
c. flavor
d. few in number

EXERCISE 3 Fill in the Blank

Use context clues to determine the word that best completes each sentence.

1. Some of the most mundane ideas contain the greatest nuggets of everyday, homespun wisdom, such as Benjamin Franklin's saying, "A house is not a home unless it contains food and fire for the mind as well as the body."

2. The sign on the classroom wall indicated that the fire marshal had determined the small, windowless room could only accommodate 20 people.

3. Will was disappointed when he learned that Kristin only wanted a platonic relationship rather than a romantic one.

4. An altruistic woman, Oprah Winfrey has provided help in fulfilling many people's dreams through her Angel Network.

5. Although making money came easily to Akeel, finding true love had proved elusive.

6. When the prescribed medication did not relieve his symptoms, Bobby worried that the doctor would think his problem was psychosomatic instead of physical.

7. Because of a hearing impairment, Sherry learned American Sign Language so she could communicate with others and thus feel less isolated.

8. Instead of expecting goodness to be inherent in their children, Heidi and Lance set specific boundaries, including requiring them to do assigned chores, having them participate in volunteer work, and limiting their exposure to media violence.

9. Although he suspected his daily routine indicated that he might be neurotic, Jeff continued to wear his lucky socks, check the fringe on the Oriental carpet to ensure that it was perfectly aligned, and use a ruler each morning to measure his sideburns while shaving.

10. Despite the myriad reasons to stay away from his ex-girlfriend's apartment, Antonio found himself standing outside her building and dialing her cell phone number with hopeful anticipation.

EXERCISE 4 Application

Using context clues, insert the vocabulary word in the appropriate blank. A part-of-speech clue is given for each vocabulary word.

As sociologists scrutinize cultural trends, a new word has emerged as a result of technology: *ludology*, the study of video game theory. Based on the Latin word *ludus* for *game*, the word was coined because of the **(1)** (adj.) myriad games people are playing for even more hours each year.

The gaming industry is one that **(2)** (v.) accommodate(s) users, not just for entertainment, but also for education, military, and business training. Although it may seem **(3)** (adj.) mundane since video games are commonplace in the daily routine of many young people, ludology is now an area that fascinates researchers from a social science perspective.

Some people believe video games are akin to the Holodek in *Star Trek* episodes in which participants can experience basic emotions **(4)** (adj.) inherent in everyone without the actual risks. Likewise, whether a relationship is romantic or **(5)** (adj.) platonic, the gamer can be in control of the outcome.

Gaming experiences can help people deal with emotional difficulties. For example, a **(6)** (adj.) neurotic person who is fearful of going to public places might use a video game to deal with anticipated fears. Also, someone with a **(7)** (adj.) psychosomatic illness can confront that fear of illness and overcome the **(8)** (n.) impairment through gaming.

When video games first appeared as entertainment, they created concern that they would be a distraction. Their benefits seemed **(9)** (adj.) elusive to many parents and educators. As more is discovered through ludology, however, sociologists and psychologists are learning that good things can come from the technology.

Video games and board games can be used by **(10)** (adj.) altruistic __________ people to help mankind or by malevolent ones to train evildoers. Like other tools, they are instrumental with many possibilities.

Stop and Think

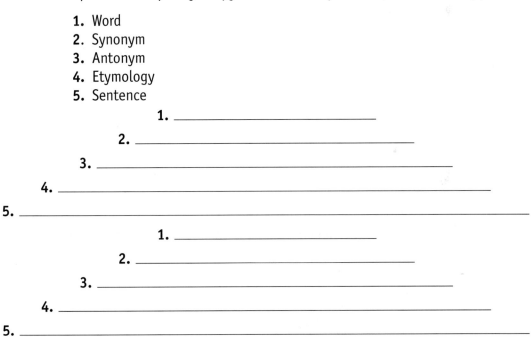

Pyramid Summary: Choose two words from this chapter and complete the pyramid summaries below. You may consult your dictionary or go to **www.dictionary.reference.com** and **www.etymonline.com** for additional help. Then compare your pyramids with a partner. (Answers will vary.)

1. Word
2. Synonym
3. Antonym
4. Etymology
5. Sentence

1. ____________________
2. ____________________
3. ____________________
4. ____________________
5. ____________________

1. ____________________
2. ____________________
3. ____________________
4. ____________________
5. ____________________

Go to **http://en.wikipedia.org/wiki/Altruism** and read the excerpt on altruism. On your own paper, write your own thoughts about the concept of altruism connecting it to someone you know, someone you admire, or something you have observed in the world. (Answers will vary.)

Vocabulary in Criminology

Get Ready to Read About Criminology

Students who pursue a degree in criminal justice take a course in criminology, which is usually a survey of the field. It includes topics in history, government, and law enforcement.

Before you read, consider what you already know about the following word parts. The meanings of some have been provided. Recall what you learned in Chapter 1 and fill in the blanks for the others.

1. The prefix *pre-* means before.
2. The root *jud* means *judgment*.
3. The root *med* means middle.
4. The suffix *-ish* means like, related to and usually indicates an adjective.
5. The suffix *-ous* means like, related to, full of and usually indicates an adjective.

attribute	cosmic	judicial	mystical	predisposition
brutish	infamous	medieval	parishioner	succumb

GOOD VERSUS EVIL

A common starting point in examining human behavior from the nonscience viewpoint is the debate over the underlying nature of humans: Do humans have a **predisposition** to good or bad behavior? The question as to whether humans are naturally bad or good has been debated in virtually every society. On the one hand, it is argued that humans are naturally selfish, evil, and violent. For example, the **medieval** political philosopher Niccolo Machiavelli (1469–1527) argued that humans, if left to their own nature, would naturally tend toward bad behaviors. He believed that humans must be controlled by rules and by threat of punishment and that behavior is determined by one's social status. The philosopher Thomas Hobbs (1588–1679) also presumed that all humans are fundamentally mean-spirited and **brutish** animals.

On the other hand, there are those who argue that humans are naturally good. Thus external control of people through law and authority is not necessary or is only minimally required. The fewer laws the better. Laws are only necessary as a guide, for it is believed that, for the most part, if left to their own instincts, humans would coexist in peace. The debate as to whether humans are born good or bad is still not settled. Classic contemporary literature, such as William Golding's *Lord of the Flies*, continues to reflect on this question.

Basic assumptions about human nature underlie the various contemporary theories that explain criminal behavior. In Western civilization, the foundation for the explanation of criminal behavior is rooted in the religious beliefs of the European Middle Ages and the Renaissance. During this time, the Catholic Church and, later, the Protestant Church were influential in defining morality and ethics in society. As a result of the strong influence of religious values on society, there was little differentiation between sin and crime. The Catholic Church was the major source of criminal law during Europe's Middle Ages, and the Church was an active agent in determining the guilt and innocence of individuals accused of breaking the law.

The common belief of people from the Middle Ages to the Age of Enlightenment was that bad behavior and thoughts were caused by sin. If asked why someone was bad, the most common answer given by people at that time would be that the person was morally weak or had **succumbed** to temptations of the world, such as greed or lust, or temptations of Satan. It could be said of this period that many people thought the reasons people committed crimes was . . . the influence of the devil.

In the American colonies, the **infamous** Salem witch trials of 1692 are a testament to the extent that people believed in evil spirits, supernatural explanations, and a **cosmic** battle of good against evil. During this time, any unusual event in one of the colonies was **attributed** to **mystical** powers, including coincidences, unusual diseases, and misfortunes. In their sermons, prominent preachers regularly warned **parishioners** of the dangers of witchcraft, satanic possession, and the Devil. In an effort to rid colonial Massachusetts of the Devil's presence, citizens used the **judicial** process as a protection against satanic influences, and this led to the witchcraft trials. Between 1672 and 1692, there were 40 cases filed involving the Devil in the Massachusetts Bay Colony. During the height of the witchcraft trials in 1692, over 150 people were arrested, 19 people were hung for practicing witchcraft, 1 was pressed to death, and 4 died while in prison awaiting trial.

—Adapted from Fagin, *Criminal Justice*, 2003, p. 73. Allyn & Bacon. Reprinted with permission.

VISUAL VOCABULARY

Many courthouses, museums, and performing arts buildings display the architecture of the __b__ period.

a. infamous
b. medieval

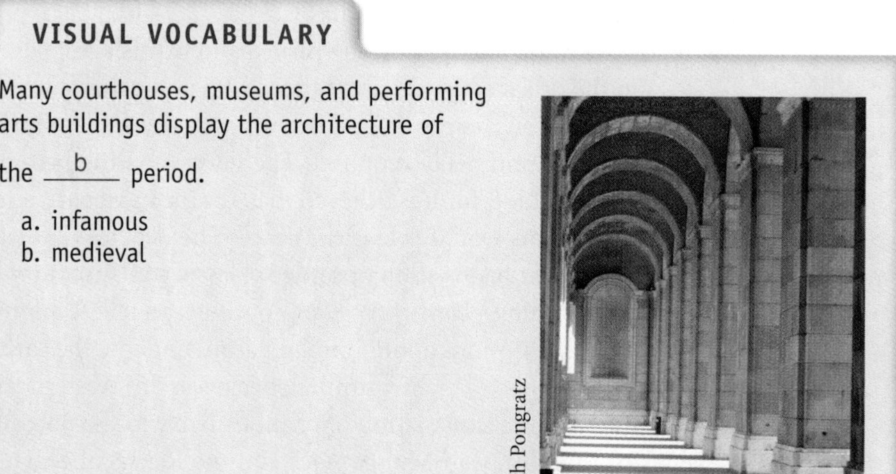

Elizabeth Pongratz

EXERCISE 1 Context Clues

Refer to the previous passage and use context clues from the sentences below to determine the definition of each of the following words in **bold** print. Do not consult a dictionary.

1. attribute (ə-trĭb′yo͞ot) v.
Althought critics complain about the negative impact of the media on America's youth, actor Tom Hanks **attributes** his fascination with acting to his family's overindulgence in viewing television so much that he was able to tell time by the programs on the air anytime during the day.

__b__ **Attribute** means
a. contact. b. credit. c. train. d. alert.

2. brutish (bro͞o′tĭsh) adj.
Sir William Wallace was portrayed in the film *Braveheart* as a courageous warrior who led his men in a **brutish** battle against the British during the 13th century Wars for Scottish Independence.

___a___ **Brutish** means
a. rough. b. secret. c. legal. d. easy.

3. cosmic (kŏz′mĭk) adj.
All of the *Star Wars* episodes depict **cosmic** battles of good versus evil.

___d___ **Cosmic** means
a. upward.
b. all-encompassing.
c. relating to challenges on Earth.
d. relating to the universe, especially distinct from Earth.

4. infamous (ĭn′fə-məs) adj.
The Hang-and-Run artist is an **infamous** and elusive character who sneaks into museums and hangs his artwork in the midst of paintings by the masters.

___d___ **Infamous** means
a. well-educated.
b. talented.
c. having an honorable reputation.
d. having a disgraceful reputation.

5. judicial (jo͞o-dĭsh′lə) adj.
The United States has three branches of government: The executive branch includes the president and staff; the legislative includes the law-makers of the House of Representatives and the Senate; and the **judicial** includes the Supreme Court justices.

___b___ **Judicial** means
a. characterized by lawmaking.
b. characterized by a court or judge.
c. characterized by showing mercy.
d. characterized by showing cruelty.

6. medieval (mē′dē-ē′vəl) adj.
Because there was no central heat, many **medieval** castles were warmed only by huge fireplaces and insulated by tapestries displayed as heavy wall hangings that also served as artwork.

___a___ **Medieval** means
a. related to the Middle Ages (A.D. 476–1443).
b. related modern times.
c. related to prehistory.
d. related to the Renaissance (14th–18th century).

7. mystical (mĭs′tĭ-kəl) adj.
Located in central Texas, the pink granite dome known as Enchanted Rock is a **mystical** place with a rich history including legends from the Tonkawa Indians about men swallowed by the rock and returning as spirits.

___c___ **Mystical** means
a. solvable.
b. simple to understand.
c. inexplicable.
d. explainable.

8. parishioner (pə-rĭsh′ə-nər) n.
When the church members realized a runaway had been living in the attic, they took up a collection and two **parishioners** volunteered to serve as foster parents until more permanent arrangements could be made.

___d___ **Parishioner** means
a. judge.
b. town council.
c. nonbeliever.
d. church member.

9. predisposition (prē′dĭs-pə-zĭsh′ən) n.
Researchers have discovered that some people have a **predisposition** to develop certain cancers, but if DNA tests can determine that tendency, then preventive measures can be introduced.

___a___ **Predisposition** means
a. inclination. b. absence. c. incorrectness. d. unsureness.

10. succumb (sə-kŭm′) v.
It has been said that doing something for 40 days can help you create a new good habit, thus avoiding the temptation to **succumb** to your old routine.

___a___ **Succumb** means
a. give in. b. avoid. c. incorrect. d. unsure.

EXERCISE 2 Word Sorts

Synonyms

Match the word to the synonyms or definitions that follow each blank.

1. ___cosmic___: universal; planetary; interstellar
2. ___attribute___: assign; account for; credit
3. ___parishioner___: lay person; believer; church member
4. ___predisposition___: inclination; bent; tendency
5. ___medieval___: ancient; relating to the Middle Ages; antiquated

Antonyms

Select the letter of the word(s) with the opposite meaning.

__a__ **6.** succumb
a. resist b. yield c. refuse d. submit

__b__ **7.** infamous
a. shameful b. reputable c. corrupt d. fearful

__d__ **8.** mystical
a. secret b. mysterious c. cryptic d. clear

__c__ **9.** judicial
a. fascinating b. alert c. law-breaking d. judgelike

__d__ **10.** brutish
a. loud b. cruel c. rough d. delicate

EXERCISE 3 Fill in the Blank

Use context clues to determine the word that best completes each sentence.

1. After exercising self-discipline for two weeks, Molly __succumb(ed)__ to the temptation of eating dessert at the new restaurant.
2. During the first week in August, people are treated to a __cosmic__ light show during the Perseid meteor showers.
3. Some people __attribute__ their ultimate success to an initial failure that prompted them to work harder.
4. An example of __medieval__ architecture is the Romanesque style that flourished during the Middle Ages.
5. One of the most __infamous__ crimes investigated by the Federal Bureau of Investigation was the Brinks Robbery in Boston, Massachusetts, on January 17, 1950, when the thieves escaped with more than $3 million in cash, checks, and money orders, only to be apprehended days later.
6. After the church burned, a journalist interviewed the minister and several __parishioner(s)__—all of whom agreed they were not bitter, only determined to rebuild.
7. Gemini seems to have a __mystical__ sixth sense because of her dreams that hint about future events.

8. Watching Emilio organize the CDs in his dorm room, we teased him that he inherited his mother's "neat" gene, a predisposition all of her children developed to create harmony from chaos and alphabetize everything in sight.

9. The judicial process of the honor code required that the students accused of cheating appear before the court and plead their cases; if found guilty, students are still allowed to appeal the decisions.

10. The room suddenly became silent when a brutish man lumbered in and bellowed the name of the bartender.

EXERCISE 4 Application

Using context clues, insert the vocabulary word in the appropriate blank. A part-of-speech clue is given for each vocabulary word.

With so many crime scene investigation television shows, it is no surprise that the interest in careers in criminology has risen. Students who want to pursue a career in forensic science, police work, probation, and homeland security are majoring in criminal justice.

In a required criminology survey course, the instructor develops a knowledge of the history of criminal justice beginning with the Code of Hammurabi, considered by some to be the foundation of the **(1)** (adj.) judicial system, moving through the **(2)** (adj.) medieval period of justice involving serfs and knights. Students learn that in each of these centuries there are **(3)** (adj.) mystical explanations for the evil people do. From the **(4)** (adj.) cosmic causes of the phases of the moon to **(5)** (adj.) infamous witches of Salem casting spells, there are outside forces to be reckoned with. Even in the Victorian period, the science of phrenology tried to predict a person's inclination to have a **(6)** (n.) predisposition to crime by the shape of his or her skull.

In addition to cause and effect relationships, students study some of the notorious criminals from the **(7)** (adj.) brutish to the bizarre.

They studied psychology to determine what causes a person to **(8)** (v.) succumb to the darker side. They also explore topics in sociology to discover trends in societies that identify deviant behavior or the reasons even loyal, church-going **(9)** (n.) parishioner(s) willingly participate in crimes.

Criminal justice students develop a number of necessary skills that are **(10)** (n.) attributed to including critical thinking and problem solving. They are detail-oriented people who like a challenge and can follow a procedure. Scientists of human behavior, they seek to explore human motivation, enforce the law, and maintain a sense of order.

Stop and Think

Write a synonym for each word below and then draw a picture that represents the word. (Answers will vary.)

brutish	cosmic	judicial
mystical	parishioner	succumb

Go to **http://www.law.umkc.edu/faculty/projects/ftrials/salem/ SALEM. HTM** and read about the Salem witchcraft trials of 1692 at "Famous American Trials." On your own paper, write a reader's response connecting your thoughts about the description to at least two words from the chapter.

CHAPTER

11 Vocabulary in American History

Get Ready to Read About American History

Most college students have some background knowledge of history if the subject was a high school graduation requirement. Consequently, college students often elect to take a course in United States or world history because of their prior studies.

In an American history course, the first semester usually begins with the pre-Jamestown period (before 1607) and follows events until the mid-19th century. In the second semester, students study the events that shaped the country from the post–Civil War until the present. Students can expect to encounter new vocabulary as well as cause and effect and sequence writing patterns.

Before you read, consider what you already know about the following word parts. Recall what you learned in Chapter 1 and fill in the blanks.

1. The prefix *con-* means with, together.
2. The prefix *pre-* means before.
3. The prefix *re-* means again.
4. The suffix *–ist* means person and usually indicates a noun.
5. The suffix *-ize* means cause to become, make and usually indicates a verb.
6. The suffix *-tion* means action, state and usually indicates a noun.

abolitionist	festoon	inflame	presumably	repeal
conservative	incur	justification	radicalize	stark

ABOLITIONISTS

The **repeal** of the Missouri Compromise struck the North like a slap in the face—at once shameful and challenging. **Presumably,** the question of slavery in the territories had been settled forever; now seemingly without **justification,** it had been reopened. On May 24, two days after the Kansas-Nebraska bill passed the House of Representatives, Anthony Burns, a slave who had escaped from Virginia by stowing away on a ship, was arrested in Boston. Massachusetts **abolitionists** brought suit against Burns's former master, charging false arrest. They also organized a protest meeting at which they **inflamed** the crowd into attacking the courthouse where Burns was being held. The mob broke into the building and a guard was killed, but federal marshals drove off the attackers.

President Pierce ordered the Boston district attorney to "**incur** any expense" to enforce the law. He also sent a revenue cutter to Boston to carry Burns back to Virginia. Thus Burns was returned to his master, but it required two companies of soldiers and 1000 police and marines to get him aboard ship. As the grim parade marched past buildings **festooned** with black crepe, the crowd screamed, "Kidnappers! Kidnappers!" at the soldiers. Estimates of the cost of returning this single slave to his owner ran as high as $100,000. A few months later, northern sympathizers bought Burns his freedom—for a few hundred dollars.

In previous cases, Boston's **conservative** leaders, Whig to man, had tended to hold back; after the Burns incident, they were thoroughly **radicalized.** "We went to bed one night old fashioned . . . Whigs," one of them explained, "and waked up **stark** mad Abolitionists."

—Adapted from Carnes and Garraty, *The American Nation*, 11th ed., pp. 372–373. Reprinted with permission.

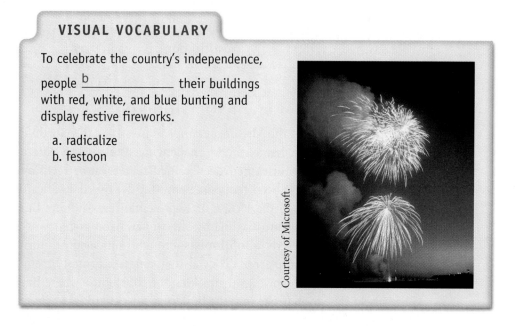

VISUAL VOCABULARY

To celebrate the country's independence, people b________ their buildings with red, white, and blue bunting and display festive fireworks.

a. radicalize
b. festoon

Courtesy of Microsoft.

EXERCISE 1 Context Clues

Refer to the previous passage and use context clues from the sentences below to determine the definition of each of the following words in **bold** print. Do not consult a dictionary.

1. abolitionist (ăb′ə-lĭsh′ə-nĭst) n.
One of the most famous books by an **abolitionist** is *Uncle Tom's Cabin* by Harriet Beecher Stowe, whose father also fought for the emancipation of slaves.

__d__ **Abolitionist** means

a. supporter of government policy.
b. supporter of slavery.
c. opponent of any government policy.
d. opponent of slavery.

2. conservative (kən-sûr′və-tĭv) n.
A **conservative** voter, Keiko prefers little or no government intervention and a limit on federal, state, and local spending.

__c__ **Conservative** means

a. environmentalist.
b. scientist.
c. one who adheres to traditional views.
d. one who adheres to nontraditional views.

3. festoon (fĕ-sto͞on′) v.
Every winter the local fifth graders **festoon** the school's evergreen tree with strings of popcorn and cranberries to create a festive way to feed the birds.

__a__ **Festoon** means
a. decorate. b. destroy. c. remove. d. finish.

4. incur (ĭn-kûr′) v.
College students are cautioned not to **incur** credit card debt because interest rates can cause a balance to increase rapidly.

__c__ **Incur** means
a. pamper.
b. announce.
c. bring upon oneself.
d. lessen.

5. inflame (ĭn-flām′) v.
Because he realized his criticism could **inflame** the state senators and rouse their anger, the governor carefully planned his speech to be assertive but not offensive.

__a__ **Inflame** means
a. excite.
b. make dull.
c. silence.
d. send away.

6. justification (jŭs′tə-fĭ-kā′shən) n.
A rubric is a tool that provides **justification** for the grade a student receives on an essay or project.

__b__ **Justification** means
a. disappointment.
b. explanation.
c. propaganda.
d. criticism.

7. presumably (prĭ-zo͞o′mə-blē′) adv.
Presumably, if you work hard, you can become wealthy; however, that is not true because many poor people are some of the hardest working people in the world.

__b__ **Presumably** means
a. under the belief that something is false.
b. under the belief that something is true.
c. in a negative manner.
d. in a disappointing manner.

8. radicalize (răd′-ĭ-kə-līz′) v.
Nothing can **radicalize** a person to act in an extreme way more than the observation of a great injustice being done to people who are too weak to defend themselves.

__a__ **Radicalize** means
a. cause extreme change.
b. prevent a change.
c. continue in a similar manner.
d. cause a small change.

9. repeal (rĭ-pēl′) v.
If Congress **repeals** the offshore oil-drilling ban, the coastlines may soon be dotted with oil rigs.

__c__ **Repeal** means
a. survey. b. establish. c. cancel. d. ensure.

10. stark (stärk) adj.
The silhouette of the bare tree branches painted a **stark** picture against the night sky.

__d__ **Stark** means
a. passive; agreeable.
b. silent; invisible.
c. unnoticeable; kind.
d. obvious; severe.

EXERCISE 2 Word Sorts

Synonyms

Match the word to the synonyms or definitions that follow each blank.

1. __presumably__ likely; apparently; probably
2. __justification__ explanation; rationale; support
3. __radicalize__ make more extreme or radical
4. __abolitionist__ slavery opponent
5. __festoon__ beautify; decorate; enhance

Antonyms

Select the letter of the word(s) with the opposite meaning.

__a__ **6.** conservative
a. liberal b. traditional c. disinterest d. partial

__d__ **7.** inflame
a. apply b. arrange c. engross d. bore

c 8. incur
a. take on b. betray c. avoid d. disperse

d 9. stark
a. alone b. rough c. simple d. ornate

b 10. repeal
a. abolish b. ratify c. vote against d. cancel

EXERCISE 3 Fill in the Blank

Use context clues to determine the word that best completes each sentence.

1. In an attempt to provide justification for his crime, the defense attorney presented the jury with a picture of his client's sad childhood.
2. After years of fitting in and trying to please everyone, Sherice radicalize(d) her life and surprised even her closest friends by her extreme ideas.
3. After everyone's departure following the funeral, Taylor was faced with the stark realization that her life would never be the same.
4. After receiving a fine for not properly closing the lid on his city trash can, Mr. LaFleur wrote a bitter letter to the editor that inflame(d) the entire city council to review the new policy.
5. "Presumably," said the professor, "anyone enrolled in this class intends to be present and prepared everyday—especially since it seems I have the reputation for being the most challenging professor on campus."
6. As soon as the bill was passed by a slight margin, its opponents gathered to seek a repeal.
7. Tamara's uncle, a conservative, was surprised when she expressed some liberal views such as her desire to protect the environment.
8. To create a quick Fourth of July parade entry, Angela and André festoon(ed) their daughter's wagon with tri-colored crepe paper and made her a costume to represent the Statue of Liberty.
9. The philosophy of the abolitionist(s) was that all human life was to be valued, and there was no justification for the enslavement of anyone.

10. The coach was a bold man who was not afraid to incur________ criticism for doing the right thing for the whole team, rather than allowing one star player to shine.

EXERCISE 4 Application

Using context clues, insert the vocabulary word in the appropriate blank. A part-of-speech clue is given for each vocabulary word.

Is it any surprise that few Americans can quote or even recognize facts from American history? This was the lament of Walter Williams, a **(1)** (adj.) conservative________ and economics professor at George Mason University. In his column, *A Minority View*, Williams noted that "a survey recently conducted by the Center for Survey Research and Analysis at the University of Connecticut gave 81 percent of the seniors a D or F in their knowledge of American history." Faced with that **(2)** (adj.) stark________ realization, Williams wrote that educators must reckon with the idea that most people cannot "identify Valley Forge, or words from the Gettysburg Address, or even the basic principles of the U.S. Constitution." According to another survey cited by Williams, more Americans can better identify the characters in the cartoon "The Simpsons" than the freedoms guaranteed by the First Amendment. **(3)** (adv.) Presumably________, these are the same people who **(4)** (v.) festoon________ their buildings with red, white, and blue bunting on the Fourth of July to celebrate Independence Day—the same people who would rebel if that independence were **(5)** (v.) repealed________ with or without **(6)** (n.) justification________.

Williams suggests the trend is the result of "phony" college courses, soft courses, and grade inflation. He also contends that such information should **(7)** (v.) incur________ the anger of parents who are paying high prices for the poor education their children are receiving.

This information, Williams hopes, could **(8)** (v.) inflame the anger of professors and parents, but he does not blame them. Instead, he said the trustees of the colleges should be held more accountable.

In the meantime, if students, parents, and professors recognize the weak background in American history, they only need to go back to the pre-Civil War period and the **(9)** (n.) abolitionist(s) who sought freedom through educating everyone. Knowledge is freedom, and remembering history and those who fought for freedom could be the motivation needed to **(10)** (v.) radicalize higher education.

—Adapted from "College Stupidity," from *A Minority View*, by Walter E. Williams. Reprinted by permission of the author.

Stop and Think

Finish the following to make a complete sentence that reveals the definition of the word. (Answers will vary; a sample is provided.)

1. Whenever I see little lights and flowers **festooned** around a garden, I think it is one of the most romantic scenes I have ever seen.
2. One thing that **inflames** me is hearing about children who suffer at the hands of those who are powerful.
3. As **justification** for his poor grades, the student blamed the teachers and the lack of organization rather than his failure to complete the assignments or study for exams.
4. If I could **radicalize** the schools, I would create small schools of the same gender that provide daily opportunities for reading and writing across the curriculum as well as the pursuit of the arts and foreign languages.

CHAPTER

12 Vocabulary in Current Events

Get Ready to Read About Current Events

Reading the editorial page of the daily newspaper requires a student to have a strong vocabulary and basic knowledge of world events and geography. Often the authors make allusions to previous news items, so staying apprised of the news is also critical. This selection is by a well-known, conservative writer, George Will, who plants the idea of some ways educators are radicalizing the system.

Before you read, consider what you already know about the following word parts. The meanings of some have been provided. Recall what you learned in Chapter 1 and fill in the blanks for the others.

1. The prefix *ana-* means against.
2. The prefix *ante-* means before.
3. The prefix *dis-* means not, separated from.
4. The root *anthrop* means humankind.
5. The root *arch* means leader, first.
6. The root *cred* means believe.
7. The root *ped* means *child.*
8. The root *phil* means love.
9. The suffix *-ate* means make, cause to become and usually indicates a verb.

10. The suffix *-ist* means person and usually indicates a noun.

anarchic	credo	emulate	pedagogy	rivet
antecedent	discern	immerse	philanthropist	tutelage

TRANSMITTING CIVILIZATION

by George Will

Los Angeles—After eight years at Robert F. Kennedy Elementary School, Ethel Bojorquez knows a thing or two about teaching. She radiates calm, no-nonsense authority, and today she is watching a kindred spirit, Carole Valleskey, put Bojorquez's 35 fourth- and fifth-graders briskly through their paces.

Actually, the paces are Valleskey's. A former ballerina with the Joffrey, she now choreographs dance classes at eight fortunate Los Angeles elementary schools. For a few hours a week Valleskey's students restrain their **anarchic** individualism in order to perform as a dance troupe. Think of training young minnows in synchronized swimming.

The children have high-energy encounters with high-quality popular culture—Ellington, Gershwin, Copland—that is a far cry from hip-hop. Bojorquez, whose experience has immunized her against educational fads, admiringly watches her pupils perform under Valleskey's exacting **tutelage** and exclaims, "They are learning about reading *right* now."

They are, she marvels, learning about—experiencing, actually—"sequencing, patterns, inferences." She explains: "You don't only listen to language, you do it."

Bojorquez and Valleskey, like all teachers, function under the tyranny of the 9/91 formula: between ages 6 and 19, a child spends 9 percent of his life in school, 91 percent elsewhere. In contemporary America, "elsewhere" means **immersed** in the undertow of popular culture's increasingly coarse distractions. In Los Angeles, where most public school pupils are Latino (Kennedy school is almost entirely Latino), "elsewhere" often means homes where English is barely spoken.

Bojorquez's raven-haired students, their dark eyes **riveted** on Valleskey, mimic her motions. These beautiful children have a beautiful hunger for the satisfaction of structured, collaborative achievement.

That begins when Valleskey, a one-woman swarm, bounces into the room and immediately, without a word of command, reduces the turbulent students to silent, rapt attention. They concentrate in order to **emulate** Valleskey's complex syncopation of claps, finger snaps, and thigh-slaps by which she sets the tone of the coming hour: This will be fun because things will be done *precisely* right.

Part Marine Corps drill instructor, part pixie, Valleskey knows that children are realists. They do not want false praise. She knows that self-esteem is the result of, not a precondition for, achievement. Her **credo** is: Every child can do it. The **antecedent** of "it" is: learn how to learn.

Her students experience a kind of freedom that is, for most children, as exhilarating as it is novel. It is not merely the absence of restraints. Rather, it is the richer freedom of a cooperative group performing to high standards within a structure of rules.

Valleskey's California Dance Institute is, essentially, Valleskey and a few teaching assistants and musicians, sustained by a few exceptionally **discerning philanthropists.** CDI is associated with, but not financially supported by, the National Dance Institute, founded by Jacques d'Amboise, for many years a leading dancer with the New York City Ballet. He was the subject of the 1983 Academy Award-winning film *He Makes Me Feel Like Dancin'*. It explored his insight that dance—the pleasures of precision, of a task done just right—serves all the **pedagogic** goals of schools.

Virtues, says Valleskey, are habits, and dance, as taught by CDI, is habituation in many of the skills of learning, as well as the components of good character. Dance, properly taught, is like sport, properly understood.

—"Transmitting Civilization" by George F. Will, from The Washington Post, March 25, 2004.

VISUAL VOCABULARY

Children learn to dance when they a__________ their teachers.

a. emulate
b. discern

Courtesy of Microsoft.

EXERCISE 1 Context Clues

Refer to the previous passage and use context clues from the sentences below to determine the definition of each of the following words in **bold** print. Do not consult a dictionary.

1. anarchic (ăn-är′kĭk) adj.
To avoid **anarchic** conditions, the president declared martial law in the city, thus establishing mandatory curfews to begin the restoration of order.

__c__ **Anarchic** means

a. orderly.
b. exact.
c. lacking order.
d. showing self-discipline.

2. antecedent (ăn′tĭ-sēd′nt) n.
After studying the new college policies, the committee decided to research the institution's history to determine the **antecedent** that led to the new rules.

__b__ **Antecedent** means

a. that which comes later.
b. that which comes before.
c. that which occurs unexpectedly.
d. that which rarely occurs.

3. credo (krē′dō, krā′dō) n.
Companies have mission statements, so it only makes sense that a person should have a written **credo** that indicates his or her personal statement of belief.

__b__ **Credo** means

a. statement of personal defense.
b. statement of personal belief.
c. complicated recipe.
d. overdue bill.

4. discern (dĭ-sûrn′) v.
The jury was directed not to make inferences, only to **discern** the guilt or innocence of the defendant based on the facts presented.

__c__ **Discern** means

a. symbolize.
b. pardon.
c. recognize.
d. remove.

5. emulate (ĕm′yə-lāt) v.
One school of thought in behavioral psychology is to study the behavior of a hero and then **emulate** that person; that is, by copying a hero's traits, a person can rise to a new level of achievement.

__a__ **Emulate** means
a. imitate.
b. discount.
c. give in to.
d. treat fairly.

6. immerse (ĭ-mûrs′) v.
Students who opt to live in the German House on campus agree to **immerse** themselves in the language since no English is spoken there.

__a__ **Immerse** means
a. absorb; engulf.
b. remove; refrain from.
c. agree; believe.
d. eliminate; ignore.

7. pedagogy (pĕd′ə-gō′jē) n.
Due to a lack of science and math teachers, some school districts are recruiting "career switchers" whose technical expertise and ability to learn **pedagogy**—that is, specific teaching strategies—have proved to be excellent instructors.

__d__ **Pedagogy** means
a. act of being a pedestrian.
b. science of treating sports injuries.
c. science of career counseling.
d. art of teaching.

8. philanthropist (fĭ-lăn′thrə-pĭst) n.
Recently, Melinda Gates, a well-known **philanthropist,** quoted an African proverb to explain the importance of charitable work by saying, "If you want to go fast, go alone; but if you want to go far, go with others."

__b__ **Philanthropist** means
a. poor person.
b. one who contributes to help humankind.
c. self-serving person who thinks of no one else.
d. stamp collector.

9. rivet (rĭv′ĭt) v.
Because the film was so intense, Antonio was **riveted** by the action and special effects; consequently, he never found an opportunity to go to the lobby for snacks.

__b__ **Rivet** means

a. release; free.
b. hold the attention of.
c. center; arrange.
d. select; nominate.

10. tutelage (to͞ot′l-ĭj) n.
Because of excellent **tutelage** by Professor Anna Rejov, a concert pianist from Prague, Selena was able to master playing Mozart's *Sonata in C Minor* during the semester.

__d__ **Tutelage** means

a. disregard. b. criticism. c. defense. d. instruction.

EXERCISE 2 Word Sorts

Synonyms

Match the word to the synonyms or definitions that follow each blank.

1. pedagogy art or profession of teaching
2. discern perceive; detect; recognize
3. tutelage education; instruction; supervision
4. credo tenet; belief; doctrine
5. emulate copy; mimic; imitate

Antonyms

Select the letter of the word(s) with the opposite meaning.

__a__ **6.** anarchic
a. orderly b. disorderly c. excited d. rough

__c__ **7.** rivet
a. fascinate b. find c. bore d. smooth

__d__ **8.** immerse
a. encompass b. absorb c. submerge d. distract

__b__ **9.** philanthropist
a. benefactor b. antagonist c. humanitarian d. patron

__a__ **10.** antecedent
a. successor b. predecessor c. ancestor d. beginning

EXERCISE 3 Fill in the Blank

Use context clues to determine the word that best completes each sentence.

1. Under the tutelage __________ of Mme. Belskis, we studied French in preparation for our study-abroad semester in Paris.
2. *Robert's Rules of Order* is a guide for parliamentarians who help prevent anarchic __________ conditions by providing advice on correct committee procedures.
3. Brain imaging has helped educators learn more about how people learn, thus showing them how to determine some of the best teaching strategies when planning classroom pedagogy __________.
4. After breaking his arm and making frequent visits to the orthopedist, Chip decided he wanted to emulate __________ his doctor and planned a career in medicine.
5. Sharing his personal credo __________, Abraham Lincoln once said, "I believe this government cannot endure permanently half slave and half free."
6. The novels of Clive Cussler rivet __________ the reader with tales of sea adventures, treasure hunting, and government conspiracies.
7. Athletic recruiters travel the country to discern __________ which athletes will be an asset to the team and succeed academically as well.
8. Shenika has been so immersed __________ in her coursework this semester that she has had very little time for a social life.
9. The antecedent __________ to many novels is the real story around which the novelist will create a fictional framework.
10. Worth more than $42 billion, investor and philanthropist __________ Warren Buffett announced in June 2006 that he would give away 85% of his fortune to the Bill and Melinda Gates Foundation, thus pledging the largest charitable donation in U.S. history.

EXERCISE 4 Application

Using context clues, insert the vocabulary word in the appropriate blank. A part-of-speech clue is given for each vocabulary word.

College students learn to become critical thinkers in their classes over a period of time with diligence and determination. That means recognizing propaganda, learning to **(1)** (v.) discern ________ fact from opinion, and identifying valid evidence. It also means discovering the leaders they hope to **(2)** (v.) emulate ________ someday because of values that parallel their own personal **(3)** (n.) credo(s) ________. As students move through courses, they notice the difference in **(4)** (n.) pedagogy ________ of professors, which often depends on the nature of the course. In some, they may become **(5)** (v.) immerse(d) ________ in a subject such as when learning a foreign language. There, they will only be allowed to speak French, for example. Other courses may be small discussion groups and the students will study under the **(6)** (n.) tutelage ________ of a professor who is considered a master researcher in that field and adept at the Socratic seminar approach.

Although some courses and teaching styles may seem **(7)** (adj.) archaic ________ and no longer applicable to the needs of the world, consider that many languages, including English, evolve from Greek and Latin roots. Also, consider that learning to communicate effectively is something that never goes out of style. Even a background knowledge of grammar (so that a writer recognizes the importance of making the **(8)** (n.) antecedent ________ of a subsequent pronoun clearly stated) helps a student become more eloquent in speaking and writing. Finally, college students develop good habits such as reading regularly so that it is not unusual for them to become **(9)** (v.) rivet(ed) ________ by the written word. Likewise, they become involved in working on community service projects, so the practice of being a **(10)** (n.) philanthropist ________ who never tires of helping to improve world conditions is second nature.

In the end, however, learning is the responsibility of the student. As Theodore Seuss Geisel (Dr. Seuss) once explained, "You can get help from teachers, but you are going to have to learn a lot by yourself, sitting alone in a room." There is no better argument for becoming an excellent critical reader and thinker.

Stop and Think

 Using at least one vocabulary word from this chapter, create a pyramid summary of the editorial "Transmitting Civilization." (Answers will vary, but a sample is provided.)

Students

at eight Los Angeles elementary

schools have been learning personal and academic discipline

through dance instruction provided by professionals who are aware that the

pedagogy teaches students rhythm and sequence that are needed for math and reading.

 Create a Frayer model by completing the blanks beneath each category.

Synonyms
altruist, benefactor
Characteristics
charity donor, humanitarian
goodhearted, generous
philanthropist
Antonyms
miscreant, malefactor
Non-examples
Hitler, Genghis Khan

UNIT 3

Review Test Chapters 8–12

3

1 Word Parts

Match the definitions in Column 2 to the word parts in Column 1.

Column 1		Column 2
f	**1.** per-	a. believe
d	**2.** psych	b. again
a	**3.** cred	c. middle
j	**4.** phil	d. mind
c	**5.** med	e. with, together
b	**6.** re-	f. through
g	**7.** arch	g. leader, first
e	**8.** con-	h. against
i	**9.** anthrop	i. humankind
h	**10.** ana	j. love

3

2 Fill in the Blank

Use context clues to determine the best word from the box to complete each sentence.

abolitionist	cognition	defiance	myriad	presumably
accommodate	conservative	incur	pedagogy	tutelage

1. Because scientists now recognize that lobsters are sentient and have cognition—that is, they can feel, think, learn, and remember—many areas now ban live lobster tanks.
2. In an act of defiance against their government's policies, a large crowd gathered to show their unity and voice their opposition.
3. The car looks small, but it can accommodate six people comfortably.
4. From the mountaintop we could see myriad constellations in the August night sky.
5. In our American Studies class, we discovered the connection between literature and history when we read the works of pre-Civil War abolitionists.
6. In the point/counterpoint section of the newspaper, the editors positioned the views of the conservative on the right-hand side of the paper and those of the liberal on the left-hand side.
7. Amanda studied under the tutelage of a former concert violinist, which was obvious by her recent professionally polished recital.
8. In preparation for her presentation on distance learning, Ruth studied the research and pedagogy for incorporating technology in the classroom.
9. Determined not to incur debt, Kyle always paid the monthly balance of his credit card.
10. Publishers are setting up programs that allow readers to browse book excerpts online; presumably, this feature is a marketing strategy to increase book sales.

3 Book Connection

Use context clues to determine the best word from the box to complete each sentence. A part-of-speech clue is provided for each vocabulary word.

adaptive	coercive	exert	mundane	resort
brutish	elusive	inherent	platonic	succumb

THE THINGS THEY CARRIED

In his novel, *The Things They Carried,* Tim O'Brien presents the soldiers of Alpha Company during the Vietnam War. He reveals their stories through items they held dear and through the narrator's memory that melds fact and fiction. One of the most acclaimed books of the genre of modern war literature, the story depicts the **(1)** (adj.) brutish__________ and violent side of fighting, the **(2)** (adj.) inherent__________ goodness of humans, the appreciation for **(3)** (adj.) mundane__________ things such as clean socks and a warm shower, and the realization that happiness and love are sometimes **(4)** (adj.) elusive__________ and worth pursuing, but hard to hold.

Some of the soldiers of Alpha Company die, which compounds the frustration and guilt felt by the survivors. Some **(5)** (v.) succumb__________ to grappling with the ghosts of the jungle after their return to the States.

The novel is a reminder of what people **(6)** (v.) resort__________ to in order to stay alive in wartime, and it attests to the **(7)** (adj.) adaptive__________ nature of humans. At the same time, it shows the devastating after-effects and **(8)** (adj.) coercive__________ nature of blurred memories that force people to carry emotional burdens.

The narrator, Tim O'Brien, and his platoon members such as Ted Lavender, Curt Lemon, and Kiowa, portray the alienation and loneliness that entrap the soldiers. Through **(9)** (adj.) platonic__________ friendships presented, the reader also discovers the importance of the connections each soldier **(10)** (v.) exert(s) ______ to create a bond.

4 Visual Connection

Write a caption for this picture using two of the words from the box.

cosmic	festoon	impairment	inflame	rivet
emulate	immerse	infamous	mystical	stark

Susan Pongratz

(Answers will vary.) ______

______

______

______

______

______

______

5 Analogies

Choose the word that best completes the analogy.

1. commend : praise :: discern : a
a. differentiate b. resort c. radicalize

2. misunderstand : fathom :: deliberate : b
a. platonic b. impulsive c. altruistic

3. confuse : clarify :: starve : b
a. festoon b. overindulge c. platonic

4. malefactor : selfish :: benefactor : b
a. impulsive b. altruistic c. adaptive

5. idea : inspire :: trait : a
a. attribute b. defy c. persist

6. trainer : athletic :: psychiatrist : __c__
a. infamous b. judicial c. neurotic

7. building : renovate :: situation : __c__
a. overindulge b. exert c. radicalize

8. fire : extinguish :: law : __a__
a. repeal b. rivet c. emulate

9. support : evidence :: reason : __a__
a. justification b. adaptation c. defiance

10. physician : medical :: judge : __c__
a. persistence b. predisposed c. judicial

UNIT 4 Vocabulary in Business, Math, and Technology

CHAPTER 13 Vocabulary in Personal Finance

Get Ready to Read About Personal Finance

Finance is a specialized major for business students who plan to work in banking, stock broking, or estate planning. Although personal finance is often a required course for a business major, it is now becoming an important focus for all college students. As you will discover in the following selection, educators recognize how a student's credit rating and knowledge of personal finance can lead to greater success after graduation.

Before you read, consider what you already know about the following word parts. The meanings of some have been provided. Recall what you learned in Chapter 1 and fill in the blanks for the others.

1. The prefix *ad-* means to, toward.
2. The prefix *de-* means down, from, away.
3. The root *fer* means carry.
4. The root *fid* means faith.
5. The root *man* means hand.
6. The root *voc,* means call.

7. The suffix *-ity* means *quality, trait* and often indicates a noun.

8. The suffix *-ize* means cause to become, make and indicates a verb.

accrue	defer	fiscal	jeopardize	mandatory
adhere	fiduciary	initiative	liability	vigilant

PERSONAL FINANCE FOR FRESHMEN

Undergrads who believe GPAs and test scores determine whether they can go to graduate school should consider another number: their credit score. Some law and medical schools encourage—and a few actually require—admitted students to submit their credit score to help the school decide if applicants have the means and commitment to complete the degree. Georgetown Law School urges students with severe credit issues to **defer** for a year while getting their finances in order. "The decisions they make today have a cumulative impact on practicing law," says Ruth Lammert-Reeves, Georgetown's assistant dean for financial aid. According to Reeves, bar examiners in states such as California and New York take an applicant's observance of **fiduciary** responsibility into consideration. The Medical College of Wisconsin even reserves the right to deny admittance if a student doesn't provide a clean credit report; otherwise, entering with a large debt may pose a **liability.**

Such actions may seem harsh, but institutions say they want to ensure that financial ignorance doesn't **jeopardize** a student's graduate education or career aspirations. "I believe we're moving into more of an advocacy role to teach them to be wise and **vigilant** about money issues and spending habits," says Anthony Sozzo, associate dean for student affairs at New York Medical College. Sozzo, who teaches a two-hour financial-planning seminar to students each year, says the school "strongly encourages students to submit a credit check upon acceptance, and 100% **adhere** to the request." A bonus: Some students have discovered credit-report errors or identity-theft issues that they were then able to correct. Undergraduate institutions are also getting in on the act of helping students develop **fiscal** responsibility. "I tell my students, you have to leave Ohio State with two products," says Tally Hart, director of financial aid at Ohio State University. "One is an excellent academic record reflecting the great course work. The second is a great financial record."

After research showed that students were much more likely to drop out of school because of "outside pressures"—such as finances and a part-time job—than poor grades, Hart developed a seven-week "Success Series." Every freshman is required to complete several sessions on such issues as debt management, academic engagement, and leadership, in order to receive credit for a **mandatory** Survey 100 class. Sessions on savings and investing, credit-card abuse, and identity theft are particularly popular. Freshmen retention has improved each year since the program was founded in 2001.

While financial-literacy **initiatives** are becoming increasingly common at U.S. colleges and universities, many schools still simply incorporate financial tips into freshman orientation and leave it at that. Such an approach isn't adequate, believes research consultant Lana Low, who interviewed 125 institutions for a financial-literacy study done for educational-consulting firm USA Funds. "I think financial literacy should become part of the fabric of an institution," Low says. She points out that financial pressures continue to build throughout students' time at college, as they often **accrue** more and more debt. Despite the various approaches schools are taking, the reality is that plenty of undergrads must learn the hard way. Their financial education begins only after having been denied a loan or forced to delay graduate studies.

—Adapted from "Personal Finances for Freshman" from Business Week Online, November 14, 2005. Copyright © 2005. Reprinted with permission of McGrawHill Companies Inc.

VISUAL VOCABULARY

Many colleges now help students learn
a ____________ responsibility as part of the academic program.

a. fiscal
b. mandatory

Courtesy of Microsoft.

EXERCISE 1 Context Clues

Refer to the previous passage and use context clues from the sentences below to determine the definition of each of the following words in **bold** print. Do not consult a dictionary.

1. accrue (ə-kro͞o′) v.
Before becoming railroad magnates, Collis P. Huntington and Mark Hopkins owned a successful hardware store in Sacramento, California, where they **accrued** wealth by selling shovels to the gold rushers in search of their fortunes.

__d__ **Accrue** means
a. settle. b. dream. c. dwindle. d. add to.

2. adhere (to) (ăd-hîr′) v.
Students are required to **adhere** to the honor code and sign an agreement during orientation indicating their understanding of the rules.

__c__ **Adhere** means
a. stray. b. visit. c. obey. d. disobey.

3. defer (dĭ-fûr′) v.
When he realized his best friend also wanted to run for president of the class, Andy announced that he would **defer** to his friend and drop out of the race.

__a__ **Defer** means
a. yield. b. avoid. c. check. d. overcome.

4. fiduciary (fĭ-do͞o′shē-ĕrē′) adj.
Emile served as the **fiduciary** guardian of his nephews and managed their trust funds with an honest attention to detail.

__c__ **Fiduciary** means
a. unfriendly.
b. friendly.
c. related to holding something in trust for another.
d. related to spending recklessly.

5. fiscal (fĭs′kəl) adj.
According to Sharon Conti, a credit union president, if students want to improve their credit rating, they can take out a loan for $500.00 and by repaying it in six months, they can improve their **fiscal** status.

__d__ **Fiscal** means
a. memory. b. physical. c. academic. d. financial.

6. initiative (ĭ-nĭsh′ə-tĭv) n.
To improve student morale, the college administration began a new **initiative** to focus on the results of a student survey of suggestions.

__a__ **Initiative** means
a. campaign. b. defense. c. lesson. d. satisfaction.

7. jeopardize (jĕp′ər-dīz′) v.
Sometimes personal obstacles rather than academic challenges **jeopardize** student success.

__a__ **Jeopardize** means
a. risk. b. strengthen. c. weaken. d. make steady.

8. liability (lī′ə-bĭl-ĭte) n.
The car needed so much work each month that it had become a financial and safety **liability** rather than an asset.

__b__ **Liability** means
a. promise; freedom. c. record.
b. burden; responsibility. d. purchase.

9. mandatory (măn′də-tôr′ē) adj.
Completion of lab work and the final project were **mandatory** requirements for passing the class.

__d__ **Mandatory** means
a. elective. b. suggested. c. optional. d. obligatory.

10. vigilant (vĭj′ə-lənt) adj.
It pays to be **vigilant** when walking across campus alone late at night.

__c__ **Vigilant** means
a. careless. b. inattentive. c. cautious. d. intelligent.

EXERCISE 2 Word Sorts

Synonyms

Match the word(s) to the synonyms or definitions that follow each blank.

1. jeopardize______ risk; hazard; imperil; endanger
2. fiduciary______ held in trust; said of paper money or the relationship of a trustee and beneficiary
3. initiative______ beginning or introductory step

4. vigilant cautious; careful; wary; attentive

5. accrue gather; acquire; collect; compile

Antonyms

Select the letter of the word(s) with the opposite meaning.

a **6.** adhere
a. disobey b. honor c. follow d. agree

d **7.** defer
a. put off b. arrange c. ignore d. hasten

c **8.** fiscal
a. monetary c. noncommercial
b. commercial d. budgetary

b **9.** mandatory
a. required b. optional c. binding d. commendable

a **10.** liability
a. asset b. hardship c. responsibility d. burden

EXERCISE 3 Fill in the Blank

Use context clues to determine the word that best completes each sentence.

1. Seth's fiscal situation changed when he signed on with a prestigious financial institution that offered an excellent benefits package and a generous signing bonus.

2. Art collectors travel worldwide to accrue masterpieces.

3. All organizations have rules to which members must adhere such as payment of dues and expectations of attendance and participation.

4. Trends in education include mandatory dress codes, required community service, and even single-gender classes.

5. A crime scene investigator learns to be vigilant for clues—ever watchful for details.

6. Campbell has the manners of a gentleman and always defer(s) to others instead of insisting on his own way.

7. Because of his previous background as an excellent driver, Hunter was determined not to jeopardize________ that record by foolishly yielding to peer pressure.

8. Through a new fundraising initiative________, the college was able to raise enough money for a new library.

9. Since his recent mistake was considered a liability________, the senator decided not to run for office again.

10. The fiduciary________ duty of a guardian is a ponderous responsibility that requires integrity and a knowledge of financial investments.

EXERCISE 4 Application

Using context clues, insert the vocabulary word in the appropriate blank. A part-of-speech clue is given for each vocabulary word.

Adria studied the profile and scenario distributed in the personal finance seminar. She had heard stories about students who **(1)** (v.) accrue(d)________ debt and **(2)** (v.) jeopardize(d)________ their **(3)** (adj.) fiscal________ standing by using several credit cards for impulsive purchases. She knew that developing the mindset of spending sprees could be dangerous, quickly reversing the acquisition of material possessions from an asset to a **(4)** (n.) liability________.

When the college began the **(5)** (n.) initiative________ to teach students to become more financially secure, the administrators explained that they viewed their role as a **(6)** (adj.) fiduciary________ duty, honoring a trust, and therefore attendance at the seminar series was **(7)** (adj.) mandatory________. In other words, participation was not an option. Each class was designed to teach aspects of personal finance, including ways to save, kinds of consumer advocacy groups, and the difference between good debt and bad debt, as well as the value of being **(8)** (adj.) vigilant________ for ways to save. Although some students did not want to **(9)** (v.) adhere________ to the requirements of the new financial literacy campaign, they eventually decided to **(10)** (v.) defer ______________ to those who knew best. At the end of the semester, students gave high marks to the program in the final evaluation, and it will now serve as a model for other colleges to replicate.

In her final reflection, Adria was one to praise the project. Due to graduate with a stellar credit rating and already some money in savings for graduate school, she has volunteered to return and talk with freshmen next year.

Stop and Think

Reread the passage "Personal Finance for Freshmen" and then, using three vocabulary words, summarize the selection in 50 words or less. (Answers will vary.)

Since **fiscal** status can be as important as test scores in higher education, freshmen are learning ways not to **accrue** the debt that can **jeopardize** their chances for academic and career success. (32 words)

Write a synonym for each word below and then draw a picture that represents each word.

accrue	adhere	defer
fiduciary	initiative	vigilant

CHAPTER

14

Vocabulary in Business Management

Get Ready to Read About Business Management

The word *management* comes from the Latin word *manus,* meaning "hand." A degree in business management requires that a student learn how to coordinate, organize, expedite, and get things done.

Before you read, consider what you already know about the following word parts. The meanings of some have been provided. Recall what you learned in Chapter 1 and fill in the blanks for the others.

1. The prefix *com-* means with, together.
2. The prefix *ex-* means from, away.
3. The prefix *un-* means not.
4. The root *mit* means *send.*
5. The suffix *-ist* means one who specializes, person, and often indicates a noun.

commerce	expertise	generalist	robust	venture
entrepreneur	facet	implement	unremitting	visionary

ORGANIZATIONAL DEVELOPMENT

Although many **entrepreneurial ventures** are started by one **visionary** individual, it is rare that one person alone can grow an idea into a multi-million dollar company. In most cases, fast-growth companies need employees and a set of business procedures. In short, all firms—new ones in particular—need an organization to efficiently **implement** their business plans and strategies. Many e-companies and firms and many traditional firms who attempt an e-commerce strategy have failed because they lacked **robust** organizational structures and supportive cultural values required to support new forms of **commerce.**

Companies that hope to grow and thrive need to have a plan for organizational development that describes how the company will organize the work that needs to be accomplished. Typically, work is divided into functional departments, such as production, shipping, marketing, customer support, and finance. Jobs within these functional areas are defined, and then recruitment begins for specific job titles and responsibilities. Typically, in the beginning **generalists** who can perform multiple tasks are hired. As the company grows, recruiting becomes more specialized. For instance, at the outset, a business may have one marketing manager. But after two or three years of **unremitting** growth, that one marketing position may be broken down into seven separate jobs done by seven individuals.

For instance, eBay.com founder Pierre Omidyar started an online auction site to help his girlfriend trade Pez dispensers with other collectors, but within a few months the volume of business had far exceeded what he alone could handle. So he began hiring people with more business **expertise** to help out. Soon the company had many employees, departments, and managers who were responsible for overseeing the various **facets** of the organization.

—Adapted from Laudon and Traver, *E-Commerce*, 2nd ed., pp. 69–70. Prentice Hall. Reprinted by permission.

VISUAL VOCABULARY

Computer programs that are marketed as more b____________ attract the attention of potential buyers who want a more powerful system.

a. unremitting
b. robust

Courtesy of Microsoft.

EXERCISE 1 Context Clues

Refer to the previous passage and use context clues from the sentences below to determine the definition of each of the following words in **bold** print. Do not consult a dictionary.

1. commerce (kŏm′ərs) n.
Early settlements were established near waterways because boats were important for transportation and **commerce.**

__d__ **Commerce** means
a. fun; enjoyment.
b. fishing.
c. popularity.
d. trade; business.

2. entrepreneur (ŏn′trə-prə-nûr′) n.
Famous **entrepreneurs** such as Henry Ford, J.P. Morgan, and Thomas Edison were known for their optimism, vision, and perseverance.

__a__ **Entrepreneur** means
a. business person.
b. generalist.
c. historian.
d. celebrity.

3. expertise (ĕk′spûr-tēz′) n.
After working in a summer internship, Adam wrote in his blog that his undergraduate knowledge had established a foundation, but he was developing **expertise** with field experience.

__a__ **Expertise** means
a. mastery. b. weakness. c. exercise. d. inadequacy.

4. facet (făs′ĭt) n.
"One **facet** of this course," explained the professor of creative writing, "is learning to develop your voice by telling your own stories."

__d__ **Facet** means
a. compound. b. fact. c. book. d. feature.

5. generalist (jĕn′ər-ə-lĭst) n.
While looking for a summer job, Angelina found an ad for a **generalist**—someone who could perform a variety of office duties—and she realized she did not have enough skills to apply.

__c__ **Generalist** means
a. someone who rarely works.
b. someone who has flexible hours.
c. someone with a broad knowledge.
d. someone with limited knowledge.

6. implement (ĭm′plə-mənt) v.
Although the design seemed good, it was too expensive to **implement.**

__b__ **Implement** means
a. pass over. b. carry out. c. neglect. d. receive.

7. robust (rō-bŭst′) adj.
The new educational product is more **robust** than previous ones, and its strength and uniqueness are major selling points.

__b__ **Robust** means
a. weak. c. simple.
b. powerful. d. difficult to use.

8. unremitting (ŭn′rĭ-mĭt′ĭng) adj.
When Crystal saw her boyfriend Jake in an embrace with another woman, she felt an **unremitting** heartache.

__a__ **Unremitting** means
a. constant. b. infrequent. c. intermittent. d. fleeting.

9. venture (vĕn′chər) n.
The Federal Trade Commission warns consumers about scams masked as get-rich-quick **ventures** such as some work-at-home schemes that include medical billing or envelope stuffing.

__b__ **Venture** means
a. inactivity. b. enterprise. c. worth. d. stillness.

10. visionary (vĭzh′ə-nĕr′ē) adj.
Visionary philanthropists believe conditions can be improved through creative thinking and hard work.

__b__ **Visionary** means
a. practical. c. unromantic.
b. idealistic; forward thinking. d. burdensome.

EXERCISE 2 Word Sorts

Synonyms

Match the word to the synonyms or definitions that follow each blank.

1. __entrepreneur__ business person; promoter; adventurer; speculator
2. __venture__ speculation; endeavor; enterprise; project
3. __facet__ aspect; angle; feature; side

4. visionary ________ dreaming; idealistic; ambitious; speculative

5. commerce ________ business; exchange; dealings; economics

Antonyms

Select the letter of the word(s) with the opposite meaning.

__c__ 6. expertise
a. knowledge b. strength c. incompetence d. clumsiness

__b__ 7. implement
a. achieve b. neglect c. observe d. cause

__a__ 8. robust
a. weak b. powerful c. fast d. circular

__d__ 9. unremitting
a. ceaseless b. tireless c. introductory d. concluding

__c__ 10. generalist
a. leader b. assistant c. specialist d. follower

EXERCISE 3 Fill in the Blank

Use context clues to determine the word that best completes each sentence.

1. Kelli decided to study business management at the local community college while she worked as an entrepreneur ________, creating a business by opening an art gallery, offering art lessons to children, and specializing in coordinating children's theme-related tea parties.
2. Although Kathy was a writing specialist, she was also a generalist ________ in many other fields because she had studied a variety of subjects at Boston College.
3. To implement ________ a good writing style, author Stephen King suggests using strong verbs and nouns and getting rid of all the adverbs.
4. "You'll soon discover," explained the software salesperson, "that our software program is much more robust ________ than your current one, and those powerful features will give you a competitive edge."
5. The new venture ________ proved profitable, and Allan realized that the risk he took by ignoring the critics would continue to prove he had good business instincts.

6. A visionary person, whether imagining a better business or political climate, must have the confidence to push for something in spite of ridicule.

7. A facet of Wes Anderson films includes flawed but endearing heroes.

8. The unremitting pleas of the two-year-old in a toy store can be annoying, but parents should learn to help children cope with the disappointment of not always getting something every time they go shopping.

9. Knowing how important it is to have a truthful résumé, Carlos pointed out that he knew AutoCad 14, but he did not yet have expertise in the latest version.

10. The state politicians debated whether or not to raise taxes to improve road conditions, since travel was a critical element of commerce, and they wanted to attract more businesses to their state.

EXERCISE 4 Application

Using context clues, insert the vocabulary word in the appropriate blank. A part-of-speech clue is given for each vocabulary word.

Kelli studied the college catalog, poring over the descriptions of several majors. Although she had previously considered studying management so that she could become a **(1)** (n.) generalist, knowledgeable in many **(2)** (n.) facet(s) of business, she had recently decided to specialize, instead, in the field of entrepreneurship. The defining moment for her came while she was researching the attributes of famous **(3)** (n.) entrepreneur(s) such as Bill Gates, Milton Hershey, and Thomas Edison. She learned that **(4)** (adj.) visionary business people such as Estee Lauder and Elizabeth Arden had certain traits in common. First, they sought to develop an **(5)** (n.) expertise and learn as much as possible about their field. Also, these entrepreneurs were risk-takers who liked the challenge of a business **(6)** (n.) venture and focused on making a profit. In addition, they were organizers who took responsibility, but they also **(7)** (v.) implemented good ideas from others and learned from past mistakes without giving up.

Kelli began making plans. She would land an internship to develop a **(8)** (adj.) robust résumé. With her **(9)** (adj.) unremitting work ethic and desire to improve the world of **(10)** (n.) commerce and trade, she would eventually be able to manage a franchise. From there, she had an idea of how to create her own business.

Stop and Think

Study the images and then write the word that best connects to each picture. Then write a sentence explaining your rationale. (Answers will vary.)

Courtesy of Microsoft.	1. commerce The umbrella term *commerce* covers a variety of trades and ways to make money.
Courtesy of Microsoft.	2. robust The character depicts a powerful and robust runner.
Courtesy of Microsoft.	3. visionary He is a visionary man who sees many possibilities.
Courtesy of Microsoft.	4. venture The businessman represents someone about to take a risky plunge, embarking on a new venture.
Courtesy of Microsoft.	5. unremitting The wave is unremitting, and it is impossible to outrun.

Select a word from the chapter and create a pyramid summary following the guidelines below. Refer to **www.dictionary.com** and **www.etymonline.com.** (Answers will vary.)

Word: ____________________

Definition: ____________________________

Word Origin: __________________________________

Antonym: ____

Synonyms: ____

Sample Sentence: ____

CHAPTER

15 Vocabulary in Statistics

Get Ready to Read About Statistics

College students are often required to take a mathematics course that is applicable to their degree. For example, statistics, which is a specialized branch of mathematics, is often required for students studying business or social sciences. In this selection, "Business Statistics," note the words that have multiple meanings, but specific applications in math.

Before you read, consider what you already know about the following word parts. Recall what you learned in Chapter 1 and fill in the blanks.

1. The prefix *com-* means with, together.
2. The root *pop* means people.

array	mean	mode	random	sample
compile	median	population	relevant	value

BUSINESS STATISTICS

The word *statistics* originally meant *state numbers*, data gathered by the government on the number of births, deaths, etc. Today the word "statistics" is used in a much broader sense to include data from business, economics, and many other fields. Statistics is a powerful and commonly used tool in business to depict **relevant** data.

In statistics, it is important to distinguish between concepts of population and sample. **Population** is the entire group being studied, whereas sample is a portion of the entire group. **Samples** should be chosen **randomly,** meaning that no one individual in the population is more likely to be chosen than is another.

An administrator, for example, might be interested in the grade point average (GPA) of all freshmen at a community college. The GPA of the entire population of freshmen can be obtained, but this might be time-consuming to **compile.** Or, if an estimate of the GPA is adequate, the administrator can randomly choose a sample of perhaps 50 freshmen and find their grade point averages. The administrator might then assume that the grade point average of this sample of students is close to that of the entire population of all freshmen.

Businesses are often faced with the problem of analyzing a mass of raw data. Reports come in from many different branches of a company or salespeople may send in a large number of expense claims, for example. In analyzing all the data, one of the first things to look for is a measure of central tendency—a simple number that is designed to represent the entire list of numbers. One such measure of central tendency is the **mean,** which is just the common average used in everyday life.

For example, suppose the sales of carnations at Tom's Flower Shop for each of he days last week were $86, $103, $118, $117, $126, $158, $149. To find a single number that is representative of this list, use the following formula.

Mean = Sum of all **values** ·/· Number of all values
For Tom's Flower Shop, the mean is

Mean = $86 + $103 + $118 + $117 + $126 + $158 + $149 = $857
$\frac{\$857}{7}$ = $122.43 (Rounded to the nearest cent)

In everyday life, the word "average" usually refers to the mean. However, there are two other "averages" in common use, the **median** and the **mode.** The median divides a list of numbers in half: one-half of the numbers lie at or above the median and one-half lie at or below the median.

Since the median divides a list of numbers in half, the first step in finding a median is to rewrite the list of numbers as an ordered **array,** or list. For example, the list of numbers 9, 6, 11, 17, 14, 12, 8 would be written in order as the ordered array

6, 8, 9, 11, 12, 14, 17

The median is found from the ordered array as explained in the following box. Notice that the procedure for finding the median depends on whether the number of numbers in the list is even or odd.

1. If the ordered array has an odd number of values, divide the number of values by 2. The next higher whole number gives the location of the median.
2. If the ordered array has an even number of values, there is no single middle number. Find the median by first dividing the number of values by 2. The median is the average (mean) of the number in this position and the number in the next higher position.

Example Find the median for the annual salaries of the following 5 employees: $12,500, $13,000, $13,200, $14,000, and $15,000.

Solution First, make sure to list the numbers from smallest to largest.
$12,500, $13,000, $13,200, $14,000, $15,000

There are five numbers in the list. Divide 5 by 2 to get 5/2 = 2.5. The next higher number is 3 so that the median is the third number or $13,200. Two numbers are larger than $13,200 and two are smaller.

The last important statistical measure of central tendency is called the mode. The mode is the number which occurs the most often. For example, 10 students earned the following scores on a business law examination.

74, 81, 39, 74, 82, 80, 100, 92, 74, 85

The mode is 74, since more students obtained this score than any other. (It is not necessary to form an ordered array when looking for the mode.)

—Adapted from Salzman/Miller/Clendenen, MATHEMATICS FOR BUSINESS, pp. 706–726,

VISUAL VOCABULARY

Reading helps students develop a(n) a ______________ of interests and enriches their vocabulary as well.

a. array
b. population

Courtesy of Microsoft.

EXERCISE 1 Context Clues

Refer to the previous passage and use context clues from the sentences below to determine the definition of each of the following words in **bold** print. Do not consult a dictionary.

1. array (ə-rā′) n.
As she planned her wedding, Sara discovered an **array** of options in themes, locations, and prices.

__a__ **Array** means
a. collection. b. disorder. c. store. d. memory.

2. compile (kəm-pīl′) v.
When composing an essay, Gina first writes a rough draft and then inserts the research she has **compiled** so that she provides the evidence from authorities.

__b__ **Compile** means
a. separate. b. assemble. c. send. d. waste.

3. mean (mēn) n.
The **mean** age of the employees surveyed at the new accounting firm was 24 years old, which means there is a great deal of youth, but not much experience.

__b__ **Mean** means
a. midpoint number.
b. average of numbers.
c. number that occurs most frequently.
d. lowest number.

4. median (mē′dē-ən) n.
To determine the validity of his test, Professor Wiedman looked at the **median** instead of the average because the middle score gave a better view of the grade distribution.

__c__ **Median** means
a. highest number.
b. most frequent number.
c. midpoint.
d. average.

5. mode (mōd) n.
In a sequence of numbers, there is no **mode** if no number is repeated.

__d__ **Mode** means
a. average number.
b. highest number.
c. midpoint.
d. most frequent number.

6. population (pŏp′yə-lā′shən) n.
When conducting a valid survey, consider the **population** you interview so that you have a balanced perspective.

__c__ **Population** means
a. interview.
b. large view.
c. entire group being studied.
d. portion of a group being studied.

7. random (răn′dəm) adj.
Although a sudoku puzzle looks like a group of **random** numbers, there is actually an organization to the arrangement.

__d__ **Random** means
a. orderly.
b. complex.
c. deliberate.
d. unsystematic.

8. relevant (rĕl′ə-vənt) adj.
With persuasive writing, remember to include only **relevant** support; otherwise, critical readers will find flaws in your argument.

__d__ **Relevant** means
a. unimportant.
b. meaningless.
c. unrelated
d. significant.

9. sample (săm′pəl) n.
Before Cameron conducted a survey for his sociology class, he decided to select a **sample** that included a wide representation of students from the campus.

__c__ **Sample** means
a. series.
b. study.
c. portion of population being studied.
d. entire group being studied.

10. value (văl′yo͞o) n.
To determine the **value** in an equation, first determine the relevant information and then decide on the function to be performed.

__a__ **Value** means
a. amount.
b. function.
c. equation.
d. application.

EXERCISE 2 Word Sorts

Synonyms

Match the word to the synonyms or definitions that follow each blank.

1. median__________ average; medium; midpoint; relating to the middle value in a distribution
2. population__________ set of individual items or data from which a statistical sample is taken
3. value__________ amount; worth; equivalent; assessment
4. mode__________ number or range of numbers in a set that occurs most frequently
5. sample__________ set of elements drawn from and analyzed to estimate the characteristics of a population

Antonyms

Select the letter of the word(s) with the opposite meaning.

__c__ **6.** relevant
a. applicable b. germane c. not applicable d. fair

__c__ **7.** compile
a. assemble b. gather c. separate d. store

__b__ **8.** array
a. collection b. disorder c. cluster d. decoration

__a__ **9.** random
a. systematic b. haphazard c. unplanned d. aimless

__d__ **10.** mean
a. balance b. compromise c. average d. maximum

EXERCISE 3 Fill in the Blank

Use context clues to determine the word that best completes each sentence.

1. Before we visit a museum, our art history class compile(s)__________ a list of the paintings we intend to see.
2. After studying an array__________ of possibilities, Nicole decided to work as a historical interpreter while saving money for graduate school.

3. Because they only wanted the views of the female population__________, the administration conducted a survey of freshmen women.

4. When advertisements report that 4 out of 5 doctors recommend their product, be sure to question the actual number of doctors in the sample__________.

5. During the trial, the judge overruled the lawyer's new evidence because it was not relevant__________ to the case.

6. After finishing the exhausting project, Anderson enjoyed relaxing and allowing random__________ thoughts to play on his mind.

7. "Ladies and gentlemen, I am here to tell you," said the professor, "that I do not measure you by the value(s)__________ of your SATs or I.Q., but by the quality of your work and the questions you ask."

8. In the sequence, 40, 50, 50, 60, 60, 70, 70, 70,100, the mean__________ is 63.3.

9. In the sequence, 40, 50, 50, 60, 60, 70, 70, 70, 100, the median__________ is 60.

10. In the sequence 40, 50, 50, 60, 60, 70, 70, 70, 100, the mode__________ is 70.

EXERCISE 4 Application

Using context clues, insert the vocabulary word in the appropriate blank. A part-of-speech clue is given for each vocabulary word.

Brett studied the general education requirements for a degree in journalism and complained, "But I won't use any of these courses. And why do I need statistics? I'm going to be a sports writer, not a mathematician."

Nothing could have pleased Dr. Spain more than to have the opportunity for a rebuttal. A statistics teacher who had volunteered to help with freshman advising, Dr. Spain was ready to explain to Brett the **(1)** (n.) array__________ of possibilities in which statistics would be **(2)** (adj.) relevant__________ to his career.

"Well, Brett, let's see. RBIs? Statistics. Yardage in a football game? Statistics. Rebounds in basketball? Statistics. If you consider the subjects sports writers tackle, you can see they must **(3)** (v.) compile__________ data, report results, and determine the **(4)** (n.) value__________ of a player's contribution to a team." She continued, "They must compute each batting average, which is the statistical **(5)** (n.) mean__________. They might need to know the **(6)** (n.) median__________, the midpoint salary of new players, to compare with both the high salaries of the stars and the lower salaries of the other rookies. Even computing the **(7)** (n.) mode__________, that number that appears most frequently, could be important."

Fascinated, Brett began to nod in agreement.

But Dr. Spain wasn't finished. "Here's a scenario. Consider the probability that you would cover the career of someone, say, of the caliber of Red Sox designated hitter David Ortiz. There is nothing **(8)** (adj.) random__________ about his success, but the fact that the Twins traded him without realizing the talent is a clue that someone had fallen short on their statistical analysis. Today, take a survey of a **(9)** (n.) sample__________ of the entire **(10)** (n.) population__________ of baseball fans, and the majority would agree that Ortiz is a favorite, a player who helped the Red Sox win the pennant."

"Okay. Okay. I'm convinced, Dr. Spain," he said with a laugh. "Not only do I need to register for the class, but I need to do well."

And that was more than a statistical probability.

Stop and Think

Finish the following to make a complete sentence that reveals the definition of the word. (Answers will vary.)

1. If you were to **compile** a list of places you hope to visit someday, it would include

   ____.

2. A **random** thought that often slips into my mind is ______________

   ____.

3. I like professors who make lectures more **relevant** by ______________

   ____.

4. The array of courses you are considering include ______________

   ____.

5. If you were to conduct a survey on campus, the sample of the population you interview would be

   ____.

Study the information at the following sites, and then write a summary and evaluation for each that indicates the benefit of using it as a reference tool.

http://www.andrews.edu/~calkins/math/webtexts/stat03.htm

The site provides an introduction to statistics with definitions and interesting points about terms such as average, mean, median, mode, midrange. In addition, there are links to follow-up lessons. This is a good reference for students who need the terms explained in another way.

http://www.amstat.org/sections/sis/career/world.html

The site provides answers to questions students may have about a career as a sports statistician, including the information most necessary: knowledge of sports, computers, and statistics.

CHAPTER 16

Vocabulary in E-Commerce

Get Ready to Read About E-Commerce

A new field that combines technology and business, e-commerce is a specialized course of study within the business departments of many colleges. The selection you will read is on the topic of security, which requires constant vigilance by merchants, thus justifying the increase in staff who have an expertise in technology.

Before you read, consider what you already know about the following word parts. The meanings of some have been provided. Recall what you learned in Chapter 1 and fill in the blanks for the others.

1. The prefix *com-* means with, together.
2. The prefix *di-* means two.
3. The prefix *dis-* means not, separated from.
4. The suffix *-ate* means cause to become, make and usually indicates a verb.
5. The suffix *-ous* means related, like, full of and usually indicates an adjective.

authenticity	compromise	dispute	render	ubiquitous
comprise	dimension	integrity	repudiate	vignette

DIMENSIONS OF E-COMMERCE SECURITY

In traditional commerce, a marketplace is a physical place you visit in order to transact. E-commerce, on the other hand, is **ubiquitous,** meaning that it is available just about everywhere, at all times.

Six key **dimensions comprise** e-commerce security: **integrity,** nonrepudiation, **authenticity,** confidentiality, privacy, and availability.

Integrity refers to the ability to ensure that information being displayed on a Web site, or transmitted or received over the Internet, has not been altered in any way by an unauthorized party. For example, if an unauthorized person intercepts and changes the contents of an online communication, such as by redirecting a bank wire transfer into a different account, the integrity of the message has been **compromised** because the communication no longer represents what the original sender intended.

Nonrepudiation refers to the ability to ensure that e-commerce participants do not deny (i.e., **repudiate**) their online actions. For instance, the availability of free e-mail accounts makes it easy for a person to post comments or send a message and perhaps later deny doing so.

A **vignette** to illustrate this would be the story of John Coffee whose online company was duped by one out of every five customers who ordered and received goods from his Coffee Sound and Communications, Inc., of Hollywood, California. They claimed they either did not authorize the purchase or receive the goods, and the credit card issuers refused to honor his **disputed** sales. As a result, he stopped taking all online credit card orders.

Authenticity refers to the ability to identify the identity of a person or entity with whom you are dealing on the Internet.

Confidentiality refers to the ability to ensure that messages and data are available only to those who are authorized to view them. Confidentiality is sometimes confused with *privacy*, which refers to the ability to control the use of information a customer provides about himself or herself to an e-commerce merchant. For example, if hackers break into an e-commerce site and gain access to credit card or other information, this not only violates the confidentiality of the data, but also the privacy of the individuals who supplied the information.

Availability refers to the ability to ensure that an e-commerce site continues to function as intended.

E-commerce security is designed to protect these six dimensions. A compromise in any of these areas will **render** a breach in security.

— Adapted from Laudon and Traver, *E-Commerce,* 2nd ed.
pp. 255–257. Prentice Hall. Reprinted with permission.

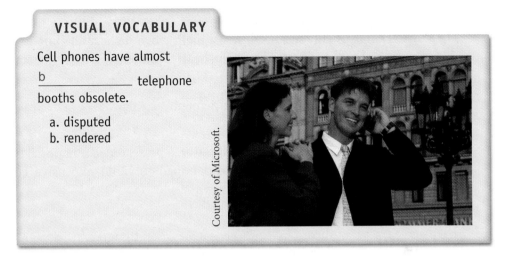

VISUAL VOCABULARY

Cell phones have almost
b______ telephone
booths obsolete.

a. disputed
b. rendered

Courtesy of Microsoft.

EXERCISE 1 Context Clues

Refer to the previous passage and use context clues from the sentences below to determine the definition of each of the following words in **bold** print. Do not consult a dictionary.

1. authenticity (ô′thĕn-tĭs′-tē) n.
Antiques Road Show presents experts who determine the **authenticity** of items, and the verification of their genuineness determines their value.

__b__ **Authenticity** means
a. fantasy.
b. quality of trust.
c. invention.
d. falsehood.

2. comprise (kəm-prīz′) v.
A course that **comprises** an online feature as well as a face-to-face lecture is known as a distributive education class.

__a__ **Comprise** means
a. consist of. b. exclude. c. examine. d. order.

3. compromise (kŏm′prə-mīz) v.
When the engineer learned that the wrong grade of steel was used, he immediately called a meeting because he knew the safety of the bridge could be **compromised**.

__b__ **Compromise** means
a. contract.
b. endanger.
c. confront.
d. disagree.

4. dimension (dĭ-mĕn′shən) n.
Ryan is usually serious, but last night when he began telling us funny stories about work, we saw a light-hearted **dimension** to his personality.

__d__ **Dimension** means
a. situation. b. settlement. c. flaw. d. feature.

5. dispute (dĭ-spyo͞ot′) v.
The local citizens who wanted the area preserved as a national historic site **disputed** with developers who hoped to build expensive condos and waterfront homes instead.

__c__ **Dispute** means
a. disorder. b. accept. c. disagree. d. agree.

6. integrity (ĭn-tĕg′rĭ-tē) n.
To preserve the **integrity** of the design, the contractor insisted on the best quality building materials.

__a__ **Integrity** means
a. soundness. b. division. c. dishonesty. d. component.

7. render (rĕn′dər) v.
At the end of the trial, the jury was directed to another room for a discussion in order to **render** a verdict.

__a__ **Render** means
a. provide. b. argue. c. expect. d. avoid.

8. repudiate (rĭ-pyo͞o′dē-āt′) v.
As expected, the politician **repudiated** any wrongdoing and cast suspicion on the staff instead.

__a__ **Repudiate** means
a. deny; reject. b. honor; accept. c. ease; relieve. d. hint; suggest.

9. ubiquitous (yo͞o-bĭk′wĭ-təs) adj.
Cell phones are **ubiquitous,** and as they continue to grow in popularity, their technology becomes more robust and more creative.

__c__ **Ubiquitous** means
a. silent. b. complex. c. being everywhere at the same time. d. rare.

10. vignette (vĭn-yĕt′) n.
At the beginning of each lecture, our sociology professor provides a **vignette** for discussion groups, and each story contains a detail from previous reading assignments.

a **Vignette** means
a. illustration. b. software. c. settlement. d. textbook.

EXERCISE 2 Word Sorts

Synonyms

Match the word to the synonyms or definitions that follow each blank.

1. entity personality; being; individual; presence

2. vignette account; description; story; anecdote

3. integrity honor; goodness; forthrightness; principle

4. dimension extent; magnitude; scale; capacity

5. comprise make up; compose; consist of; constitute

Antonyms

Select the letter of the word(s) with the opposite meaning.

d **6.** ubiquitous
a. accidental b. talented c. ever-present d. scarce

c **7.** repudiate
a. suspect b. disown c. forgive d. banish

a **8.** authenticity
a. lie b. fact c. business d. truth

b **9.** compromise
a. endanger b. protect c. order d. hesitate

b **10.** dispute
a. disagree b. go along c. alarm d. question

EXERCISE 3 Fill in the Blank

Use context clues to determine the word that best completes each sentence.

1. Coaches and guidance counselors encourage high school students to study the requirements that comprise the eligibility of an NCAA athlete.

2. A handwriting expert was called in to determine the authenticity________ of a signature on a check.

3. Nicole's lab partner generously rendered________ assistance to other students since she had developed a wide array of information about biology in her summer job.

4. A mediator was hired to help the two parties who were disputing________ over the new salary and benefits package.

5. Refusing to compromise________ her high standards, Shirley worked additional hours off-contract to make sure the project was completed with excellence.

6. Although rare in many areas, armadillos are ubiquitous________ in the Southwest.

7. When it was determined the mayor had accepted bribes, he was repudiated________ by the media.

8. Scientists follow the procedures of the scientific method to preserve the integrity________ of each experiment.

9. With each painting, Dr. Durrette, our art history professor, told a brief vignette________ to help us remember the significance of the work to its time period.

10. When the story first appeared in the news, few people could predict the dimension________ of the effect it would have on the employees who had lost their life savings.

EXERCISE 4 Application

Using context clues, insert the vocabulary word in the appropriate blank. A part-of-speech clue is given for each vocabulary word.

Professor Dixon scanned the room of new students and began his lecture. "We've come a long way from the days of trading beads or shipping tobacco to Europe for commerce," he said. "That is a fact that we cannot **(1)** (v.) repudiate________. Indeed, many new facets of trade now **(2)** (v.)

comprise ________ the current business world, which has an even more global perspective."

Then Professor Dixon posed a question. "What do you think has had the greatest impact on world trade in the past decade?"

"Computers?" queried one student.

"Absolutely. Computers have become more **(3)** (adj.) ubiquitous ________, and they have **(4)** (v.) rendered ________ our old ways of doing business out of date. Let me give you a **(5)** (n.) vignette ________ to illustrate."

Then he began with a real life story.

"As a young man, Charles Correll learned the art of glassblowing while working at a summer job at the glasshouse on Jamestown Island. Although he earned a psychology degree in college, he decided that glassblowing enhanced the creative **(6)** (n.) dimension ________ in his life—an aspect he hoped to develop. As a result, he studied under some masters in the art world and perfected his own style.

Correll also learned that turning a profit with art can be unpredictable, so he drew on another talent he had developed in physics class. He invented a furnace design that was more gas-efficient. Also, he used only the best materials to preserve the **(7)** (n.) integrity ________ of his product. Correll saw this as a practical avenue to continue creating as a craftsman and inventor.

What made the marriage of the art and scientific world more lucrative for him, however, was the Internet. Through his Web site, e-mail, and instant messaging, he has been able to create a business that takes him to the far corners of the world to teach, install furnaces, and sell his art glass.

As a result, no one can **(8)** (n.) dispute ________ the success Correll has achieved. He has lived his life with **(9)** (n.) authenticity ________, staying true to his calling, and also proving that doing business from a studio in rural western Massachusetts is possible. Because he was unwilling to **(10)** (v.) compromise ______ his personal vision, he leads a life of contentment and creativity.

Stop and Think

Write a synonym for each word below and then draw a picture that represents the word. (Answers will vary.)

dimension	dispute	render
repudiate	ubiquitous	vignette

Complete the Frayer model for the word *integrity* by adding to each category.

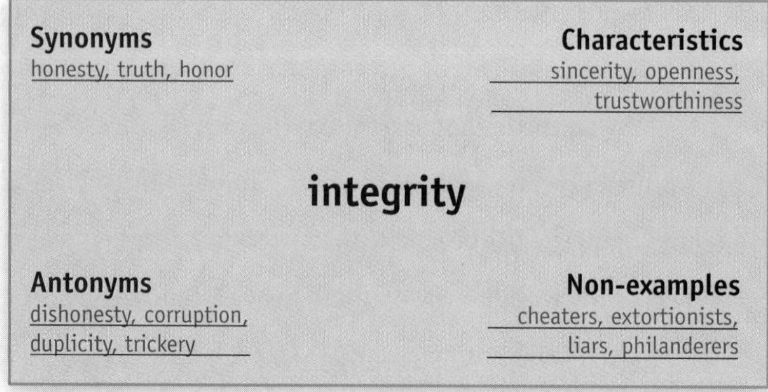

Synonyms
honesty, truth, honor
Characteristics
sincerity, openness, trustworthiness
integrity
Antonyms
dishonesty, corruption, duplicity, trickery
Non-examples
cheaters, extortionists, liars, philanderers

CHAPTER

17

Vocabulary in Computer Technology

Get Ready to Read About Computer Technology

As computers become more ubiquitous, consumers need to develop a foundation of how to protect their programs and equipment from viruses and hackers. This selection on spyware deals with a problem that is central to the security of both business and home computers.

Before you read, consider what you already know about the following word parts. The meanings of some have been provided. Recall what you learned in Chapter 1 and fill in the blanks for the others.

1. The prefix *ex-* means from, away.
2. The root *sag* means wise.
3. The suffix *-ent* means *one who, one that.*
4. The suffix *-ous* means *like, related, full of* and usually indicates an adjective.

barrage	deleterious	firewall	plethora	salient
browser	exploit	patch	sagacious	savvy

SPYWARE

Just when you thought you were Web **savvy,** one more privacy, security, and functionality issue crops up—spyware. Installed on your computer without your consent, spyware software monitors or controls your computer use.

It may be used to send you a **plethora** of pop-up ads, redirect your computer to websites, monitor your Internet surfing, or record your keystrokes, which, in turn, could lead to identity theft.

Many experienced Web users have learned how to recognize the **salient** features of spyware, avoid it, and delete it. According to the Federal Trade Commission (FTC), the nation's consumer protection agency, all computer users should take a more **sagacious** approach and recognize the signs that spyware has been installed on their machines, and then take the appropriate steps to delete it.

The clues that spyware is on a computer include:

- a **barrage** of pop-up ads
- a hijacked **browser**—that is, a browser that takes you to sites other than those you type into the address box
- a sudden or repeated change in your computer's Internet home page
- new and unexpected toolbars
- new and unexpected icons on the system tray at the bottom of your computer screen
- keys that don't work (for example, the "Tab" key that might not work when you try to move to the next field in a Web form)
- random error messages
- sluggish or downright slow performance when opening programs or saving files

The good news is that consumers can take steps to lower their risk of spyware infections. Indeed, experts at the FTC and across the technology industry suggest that you:

- Update your operating system and Web browser software. Your operating system (like Windows or Linux) may offer free software "**patches**" to close holes in the system that spyware could **exploit.**
- Download free software only from sites you know and trust.
- Don't install any software without knowing exactly what it is.
- Minimize "drive-by" downloads. Make sure your browser security setting is high enough to detect unauthorized downloads, for example, at least the "Medium" setting for Internet Explorer. Keep your browser updated.
- Don't click on any links within pop-up windows. If you do, you may install spyware on your computer. Instead, close pop-up windows by clicking on the "X" icon in the title bar.
- Don't click on links in spam that claim to offer anti-spyware software. Some software offered in spam actually installs spyware that will have a **deleterious** effect on your computer.

- Install a personal **firewall** to stop uninvited users from accessing your computer. A firewall blocks unauthorized access to your computer and will alert you if spyware already on your computer is sending information out.

If you think your computer might have spyware on it, experts advise that you take three steps: Get an anti-spyware program from a vendor you know and trust. Set it to scan on a regular basis—at least once a week—and every time you start your computer, if possible. And delete any software programs the anti-spyware program detects that you don't want on your computer.

—Adapted from "Spyware," *Federal Consumer Alert*, http://www.ftc.gov/bcp/menu-internet.htm, retrieved July 18, 2006.

VISUAL VOCABULARY

Avoid eating foods that could be a__________ to your health, and include healthful meals instead.

a. deleterious
b. savvy

Courtesy of Microsoft.

EXERCISE 1 Context Clues

Refer to the previous passage and use context clues from the sentences below to determine the definition of each of the following words in **bold** print. Do not consult a dictionary.

1. barrage (bə-räzh′) n.
After a **barrage** of questions from reporters, the spokesperson said, "Thank you all for coming; that will be all."

__c__ **Barrage** means
a. border. b. ship. c. flood. d. trickle.

2. browser (brou′zər) n.
When she was not able to find anything in her Internet search through MSN, Sandy decided to switch to another **browser.**

__c__ **Browser** means
a. online shopping feature.
b. computer security device.
c. program that accesses Internet data.
d. program that fixes computer problems.

3. deleterious (dĕl′-ĭ-tîr′-əs) adj.
Because of their **deleterious** effects, nutritionists recommend curbing the intake of sugar and fat and increasing consumption of fruits, vegetables, beans, and grains.

__a__ **Deleterious** means
a. harmful.
b. helpful.
c. advantageous.
d. dull.

4. exploit (ĕk′sploit′) v.
Sasha quit her job when she realized her employer had **exploited** her by paying her less than the other workers but requiring her to do more.

__b__ **Exploit** means
a. treat fairly.
b. use selfishly.
c. honor respectfully.
d. distinguish nobly.

5. firewall (fīr wôl′) n.
To protect his computer from hackers, Giles installed a new **firewall.**

__d__ **Firewall** means
a. program that accesses Internet data.
b. online shopping feature.
c. program that fixes computer problems.
d. security measure to prevent hackers.

6. plethora (plĕth′ ar-ə) n.
Isabel opened the large Crayola box to find a **plethora** of colors.

__d__ **Plethora** means
a. pleasure.
b. art.
c. lack.
d. abundance.

7. patch (păch) n.
To fix a new problem that occurred with his computer, Jack downloaded and installed a **patch** that had been created to eliminate the virus.

__a__ **Patch** means
a. program that fixes computer problems.
b. program that prevents hackers.
c. program included with a computer purchase.
d. security measure for online shopping.

8. sagacious (sə-gā′shəs) adj.
Jeff made a financially **sagacious** decision when he bought *Google* stock the first day it went on the market.

__b__ **Sagacious** means
a. reckless.
b. smart.
c. risky.
d. careful.

9. salient (sāl ē-ant) adj.
Emily cringed when recalling the most **salient** memory connected to the topic selected by her creative nonfiction professor: Shame.

__a__ **Salient** means
a. noticeable.
b. smooth.
c. inconspicuous.
d. unimportant.

10. savvy (săv′ē) adj.
Becoming more fiscally **savvy** is one of Gail's personal goals.

__a__ **Savvy** means
a. talented.
b. untrained.
c. not skilled.
d. rich.

EXERCISE 2 Word Sorts

Synonyms

Match the word to the synonyms or definitions that follow each blank.

1. firewall ______ security measure to prevent unauthorized monitoring of your computer
2. salient ______ significant; striking; noticeable; obvious
3. barrage ______ mass; profusion; deluge; bombardment
4. browser ______ program that accesses files and displays data available on the Internet
5. patch ______ piece of code added to software to fix a problem

Antonyms

Select the letter of the word(s) with the opposite meaning.

__a__ 6. plethora
a. lack b. excess c. happiness d. overflow

__c__ 7. savvy
a. simple b. sensitive c. unskilled d. skillful

__d__ 8. deleterious
a. corrupt b. excessive c. harmful d. beneficial

__b__ **9.** exploit
a. misuse b. treat fairly c. manipulate d. accomplish

__c__ **10.** sagacious
a. smart b. tender c. foolish d. wise

EXERCISE 3 Fill in the Blank

Use context clues to determine the word that best completes each sentence.

1. "The standard procedure in the office," explained the technical support supervisor to the new intern, "is to check weekly downloads for any security __patch__ that is available to fix new problems that arise."
2. The __sagacious__ grandfather was the family patriarch, the person everyone turned to for advice.
3. Employers often look for new candidates who are computer __savvy__ since that expertise enhances the efficiency of the company.
4. Price gouging that occurred after the earthquake is one example of how merchants __exploit__ members of a community.
5. After meeting Alissa, Sam sent her a __barrage__ of emails, hoping one of the letters would convince her to go out with him.
6. Lance collected a __plethora__ of CDs over many years, and subsequently decided to start a part-time business as a disc jockey.
7. Once doctors realized that asbestos was __deleterious__ to a person's lungs, the material was no longer used in home construction even though it is nonflammable.
8. Some popular __browser(s)__ for searching the Web include Google, Yahoo, and Dogpile.
9. Employers install __firewall(s)__ and filters based on the needs of the company and to hinder employees from using computers for personal entertainment.
10. The student became a __salient__ feature in the lecture hall because of his numerous, albeit insightful, questions.

EXERCISE 4 Application

Using context clues, insert the vocabulary word in the appropriate blank. A part-of-speech clue is given for each vocabulary word.

In the past few decades computers have become more prevalent in the world. A **(1)** (adj.) salient __________ part of many businesses and homes, they encourage efficiency and better communication. For some people, however, expressing thoughts is still a challenge.

Can you imagine what it would be like to have great ideas but no way to express them? What if you have a **(2)** (n.) barrage __________ of questions, but you have to keep them to yourself because of your communication limitations?

Richard Ellenson, an advertising executive, has been aware of such frustration because of watching his son Thomas, who suffers from the **(3)** (adj.) deleterious __________ effects of cerebral palsy. As a result of Thomas's communication challenges, his father began to think of ways to remedy the problem. This led to the creation of *Tango*, a kid-friendly computer communication device.

Unlike other communication programs, *Tango* provides a **(4)** (n.) plethora __________ of responses that are real comments a child would make, such as, "Dad, you're bugging me." Also, the voice is in a natural speech pattern, rather than an automated, belabored voice of a robot.

As computer experts become more **(5)** (adj.) savvy __________ about creating **(6)** (n.) firewall(s) __________ to protect from hackers, **(7)** (n.) patch(es) __________ to fix new problems that arise, or even more robust **(8)** (n.) browser(s) __________ that help us surf the Internet more efficiently, it is comforting to know that not everyone is trying to **(9)** (v.) exploit __________ the market as a self-serving profiteer. Instead, technology can improve the quality of life for everyone. A **(10)** (adj.) sagacious __________ father, Ellenson explains about his new device, "If there's one thing I want to change in the world, it's to assume someone in a wheelchair has a headline over their head which does not say, 'My life is difficult' but says, 'My life is interesting. My life is fun.' And in some cases, 'My life is triumphant.'"

—Adapted from ABC Nightly News, Person of the Week, Richard Ellenson, July 28, 2006. Reprinted courtesy of ABCNEWS.com.

Stop and Think

Multiple Meanings. Use your dictionary or **www.dictionary.com** to consider the meanings that apply in other career fields.

1. *firewall:* a fireproof wall used to prevent the spread of a fire—fire science
2. *browser:* a person who is looking without interest in anything in particular—business/marketing
3. *patch:* dressing for an injury: medicine
4. *patch:* cloth badge affixed to a garment for decoration: military science

Go to **www.etymonline.com** and research the origins and meanings of the following words. Complete the summaries by filling in the blanks.

1. *deleterious:* First appearing in English in 1693, the word has Greek origins from words that mean "destroyer" and "to hurt, injure."
2. *exploit:* Earlier uses of the word related it to the word explicit in the sense of something unfolding. The definition "to use selfishly" appeared around 1838.
3. *plethora:* In 1541, the word was used in the medical sense to refer to bodily fluids. It evolved in the early 1700s to mean "overfullness."
4. *savvy:* In 1785, the word arose from West Indian pidgin from the French phrase *savez vous?* which means "Do you know?" and was later used as an adjective in 1905.

UNIT 4

4

Review Test
Chapters 13–17

1 Word Parts

A. Match the definitions in Column 2 to the word parts in Column 1.

Column 1		Column 2
j	**1.** ad-	a. faith
e	**2.** fer	b. not
a	**3.** fid	c. wise
g	**4.** man	d. people
i	**5.** -ate	e. carry
b	**6.** un	f. two
d	**7.** pop	g. hand
f	**8.** di-	h. send
c	**9.** sag	i. cause to become; make
h	**10.** mit	j. to, toward

2 Fill in the Blank

Use context clues to determine the best word from the box to complete each sentence.

accrue	compromise	facet	mandatory	robust
authenticity	expertise	liability	mean	sample

1. A financial planner helps clients accrue ______ wealth through investments and a disciplined savings plan.
2. By studying the batting averages of the players, the team statistician recommended the best player for the position of designated hitter based on his position in comparison to the mean ______ scores.
3. The archaeologist confirmed the authenticity ______ of the jewelry, and the museum curator immediately arranged for a press conference.
4. The Information Technology team realized that security had been compromise(d) ______ when their computers kept receiving unauthorized pop-ups that interfered with the programs.
5. The college was surprised when the scientist offered to be a consultant and share his expertise ______ without expectation of compensation.
6. "As the co-signer of the loan," explained the realtor, "you accept the liability ______ if something happens, and you will have to pay for any overdue rent or repairs."
7. According to the new policy, parking decals are mandatory ______, and you should take care of that requirement at the beginning of the semester to avoid getting a fine.
8. We questioned the results of the survey to determine the company's eligibility to be on the Fortune 500 list when we discovered that only vice-presidents were interviewed and no other employees were included in the sample ______.
9. A facet ______ of writing-across-the-curriculum programs is that professors in all disciplines are trained to work on students' writing skills.
10. The software company announced that after years of anticipation, the powerful new operating system was more robust ______ and more secure.

3 Book Connection

Use context clues to determine the best word from the box to complete each sentence. A part-of-speech clue is provided for each vocabulary word.

adhere	implement	random	render	value
deleterious	integrity	relevant	repudiate	visionary

KINDRED

When Dana suffers dizziness in her 1970s California home and suddenly finds herself on a riverbank saving a drowning child, she does not realize at first that she has time-traveled to the 19th century antebellum South. Arriving in pre-Civil War Maryland, she discovers information that proves **(1)** (adj.) deleterious to the safety of the young African American who can read and write and compute to determine the **(2)** (n.) value of equations—all of which slaves were forbidden to do. Ironically, everything she had learned about American history quickly becomes more **(3)** (adj.) relevant, especially during subsequent **(4)** (adj.) random visits.

As suddenly as she is whisked to the past, she becomes a slave and must **(5)** (v.) adhere to the rules of the plantation owner. The owner's son, Rufus, the young boy Dana initially saved from drowning, matures with each of her visits. Unfortunately, Rufus grows to emulate his father—a man who lacks **(6)** (n.) integrity, compassion, or decency. In spite of Dana's efforts to encourage the inherent goodness in Rufus, he eventually **(7)** (v.) repudiate(s) her and her intelligence over his own fear and lack of education. Still, Dana must find a way to keep Rufus alive until he sires a child who will become one of her ancestors. Otherwise, Dana will cease to exist. She must also try to find a way back to her present and avoid continually being whooshed back in time.

Octavia Butler did extensive research on slave narratives to **(8)** (v.) render______ an authentic framework for *Kindred*. Known as a **(9)** (adj.) visionary______ writer and one of the only African American science fiction novelists, Butler carefully wove a credible story, adeptly **(10)** (v.) implement(ing)______ the rules of the time-travel genre, and creating a story now considered a classic.

4 Visual Connection

Write a caption for this picture using two of the words from the box.

array	comprise	fiduciary	initiative	ubiquitous
commerce	entrepreneur	fiscal	plethora	venture

Elizabeth Pongratz

(Answers will vary.)

5 Analogies

Choose the word that best completes the analogy.

1. total votes : popularity :: frequency : ___c___
   a. patch b. mean c. mode

2. events : unplanned :: thoughts : ___c___
   a. robust b. savvy c. random

3. skill : adeptness :: knowledge : ___a___
   a. savvy b. ubiquitous c. deleterious

4. citizens : prominent :: characteristics : ___b___
   a. vigilant b. salient c. mandatory

5. cover : paint :: fix : ___a___
   a. patch b. mode c. median

6. destroy: virus :: protect : ___c___
   a. venture b. sample c. firewall

7. view : lens :: search : ___a___
   a. browser b. dimension c. population

8. excerpt : selection :: story : ___c___
   a. venture b. array c. vignette

9. some : few :: many : ___b___
   a. patch b. barrage c. median

10. careless : inattentive :: cautious : ___c___
    a. mandatory b. relevant c. vigilant

UNIT 5 Vocabulary in Communications and Humanities

CHAPTER 18 Vocabulary in Interpersonal Communication

Get Ready to Read About Interpersonal Communication

A course in interpersonal communication includes topics in cultural differences, verbal and nonverbal communication, listening styles, body language, friendship, and love. In this selection, you will read a selection about power and one of the often quoted power authorities.

Before you read, consider what you already know about the following word parts. The meanings of some have been provided. Recall what you learned in Chapter 1 and fill in the blanks for the others.

1. The prefix *con-* means with, together __________.
2. The prefix *pro-* means for, forward __________.
3. The root *equ* means *equal.*
4. The root *gen* means *birth, kindred.*
5. The root *man* means hand __________.
6. The root *voc* means call __________.

7. The suffix *-al* means *like, related to* and indicates an adjective.

8. The suffix *-ive* means *of, like, related to, being* and indicates an adjective.

9. The suffix *-tion* means action, state and indicates a noun.

acquiesce	congenial	manipulative	propensity	substantiate
conducive	equivocal	orientation	strategy	wield

POWER

Niccolo Machiavelli (1469–1527) was a political philosopher and advisor who wrote his theory of political control in *The Prince.* Machiavelli asserted that the prince must do whatever is necessary to rule the people; the ends justify or **substantiate,** the means. The ruler was in fact obligated to use power and thus achieve the desired goals. The term *Machiavellian* has thus come to refer to the techniques or tactics one person uses to control another person. Research finds significant differences between those who score high and those who score low on the Mach scale (an attitude assessment scale). Low Machs are more easily persuaded; high Machs are more resistant to persuasion. Low Machs are more empathic; high Machs are more logical. Low Machs are more interpersonally oriented and involved with other people; high Machs are more assertive and more controlling. Business students (especially marketing students) score higher in Machiavellianism than do nonbusiness majors.

Machiavellianism seems, in part at least, to be culturally conditioned. Individualist **orientation,** which favors competition and being Number One, seems more **conducive** to the development of Machiavellianism. Collectivist orientation, which favors a **propensity** toward cooperation, a willingness to **acquiesce** and being one of the group, seems a less **congenial** environment for the development of Machiavellianism in its members. Some evidence of this comes from research showing that Chinese students attending a traditional Chinese (Confucian) school rated lower in Machiavellianism than similar Chinese students attending a Western-style school. Age is also related to Machiavellianism. Younger people score significantly higher on Machiavellianism than older people.

Your level of Machiavellianism will influence the communication choices you make. For example, if you were a high Mach, you would be more strategic, **equivocal,** and **manipulative** in your self-disclosures and in your conflict-solving **strategies** than you would be if you were a low Mach. High Machs are generally more effective in just about all aspects studied—they even earn higher grades in communication courses that involve face-to-face interaction. Low Mach women, however, are preferred as dating partners by both high and low Mach men.

Although people differ greatly in the amount of power they **wield** at any time and in any specific area, everyone can increase their power in some ways. You can lift weights and increase your physical power. You can learn the principles of communication and increase your persuasive power.

—Adapted from Devito *The Interpersonal Communication Book,* 10th ed., pp. 335–337. Allyn & Bacon. Reprinted with permission.

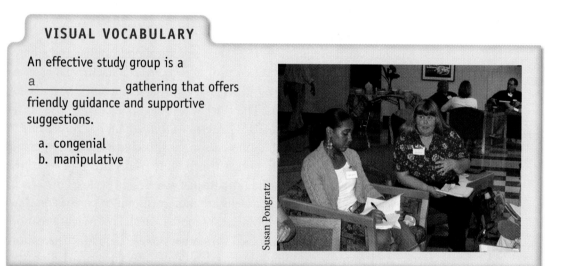

VISUAL VOCABULARY

An effective study group is a a______ gathering that offers friendly guidance and supportive suggestions.

a. congenial
b. manipulative

Susan Pongratz

EXERCISE 1 Context Clues

Refer to the previous passage and use context clues from the sentences below to determine the definition of each of the following words in **bold** print. Do not consult a dictionary.

1. acquiesce (ăk′wē-ĕs′) v.
The advanced composition course taught Sandra to find her voice in writing, and at the same time, she learned that she did not always have to **acquiesce** to keep people happy.

d **Acquiesce** means

a. manage carelessly.
b. attempt to be unclear.
c. avoid the truth.
d. agree passively.

2. conducive (kən-do͞o′sĭv) adj.
Listening to music while studying can be **conducive** to good concentration as long as there are no accompanying lyrics to distract you.

__c__ **Conducive** means
a. unfavorable. b. harmful. c. helpful. d. problematic.

3. congenial (kən-jēn′yəl) adj.
Dr. Alvarez is a **congenial** man who smiles often and playfully begins each class with a joke.

__c__ **Congenial** means
a. impolite. b. prompt. c. friendly. d. disagreeable.

4. equivocal (ĭ-kwĭv′ə-kəl) adj.
It is frustrating to talk to Owen because he is so charming, yet **equivocal,** and I'm never sure when he is telling the truth.

__a__ **Equivocal** means
a. unclear; ambiguous. c. accurate.
b. clear; unambiguous. d. certain.

5. manipulative (mə-nĭp′yə-lə-tĭv) adj.
Although Tiffany was a **manipulative** woman, Ted loved her, even when he knew she was always trying to get her own way.

__d__ **Manipulative** means
a. honest. b. reckless. c. soothing. d. scheming.

6. orientation (ôr′ē-ĕn-tā′shən) n.
The **orientation** for a new job is often stressful because a new employee is introduced to and expected to learn about myriad policies, people, and procedures.

__b__ **Orientation** means
a. confusion. b. adaptation. c. avoidance. d. admiration.

7. propensity (prə-pĕn′sĭ-tē) n.
Mike's **propensity** for beautiful women earned him the reputation of a "polyamorous himbo."

__d__ **Propensity** means
a. weakness. b. distaste. c. coldness. d. inclination.

8. strategy (străt′ə-jē) n.
Akeel developed a **strategy** of essay writing that involved using colored highlighters to indicate the main idea, details, and transition words.

__a__ **Strategy** means
a. plan. b. honesty. c. disorder. d. excuse.

9. substantiate (səb-stăn′shē-āt′) v.
"There is no way to **substantiate** the actions of your mistreatment of Colleen," said Jan, "but you can apologize and ask her to forgive you."

__a__ **Substantiate** means
a. excuse. b. confuse. c. attack. d. aid.

10. wield (wēld) v.
Minnesota is the home of the legendary Babe, the Blue Ox and Paul Bunyan, who could **wield** an axe better than any other logger.

__d__ **Wield** means
a. straighten. b. follow. c. lower. d. control.

EXERCISE 2 Word Sorts

Synonyms

Match the word to the synonyms or definitions that follow each blank.

1. wield use; handle; manage; operate
2. conducive promoting; helpful; useful; contributory
3. orientation adjustment; bearings; adaptation; direction
4. substantiate rationalize; justify; give reasons for; account for
5. strategy plan; tactic; scheme; method

Antonyms

Select the letter of the word(s) with the opposite meaning.

__b__ **6.** congenial
a. friendly b. unfriendly c. kind d. charitable

__a__ **7.** acquiesce
a. disagree b. claim c. declare d. advise

__c__ **8.** propensity
a. tendency c. avoidance or aversion
b. bias d. bent

__a__ **9.** manipulative
a. honest b. scheming c. planning d. difficult

d 10. equivocal
a. vague b. untruthful c. lying d. honest

EXERCISE 3 Fill in the Blank

Use context clues to determine the word that best completes each sentence.

1. After a week of orientation consisting of meetings and registration, the freshmen were ready for the first day of class.
2. A good strategy for making a speech is to begin with a humorous anecdote, which encourages the audience to laugh and relax.
3. An intelligent woman, the secretary of state wield(s) her power, yet remains cool and determined under pressure.
4. An equivocal answer is not a lie, but because it is so vague, the truth is difficult to determine.
5. Everyone on campus is committed to creating a congenial atmosphere, and they greet each visitor with a smile.
6. "Driving a car that leaks and has no heater," complained Jim, "is not conducive to getting a date."
7. Being passive/aggressive is a manipulative and unkind tactic to get your way without voicing your feelings.
8. Because of her propensity for oversleeping, Faye sets four alarms five minutes apart.
9. In order to substantiate his reasons for buying a new car, Roger explained that he could save on fuel and maintenance costs with a more recent model.
10. Instead of trying to acquiesce and always express agreement with his co-workers, Tyler began to voice his opinions more clearly at meetings.

EXERCISE 4 Application

Using context clues, insert the vocabulary word in the appropriate blank. A part-of-speech clue is given for each vocabulary word.

Recognizing the role of spoken and unspoken language has a prominent place in all levels of communication in the animal kingdom. For humans, the differences in unspoken communication varies with the **(1)** (n.) orientation of a person's particular culture. Southern Europeans take up personal space and maintain eye contact with others, whereas people from Asian cultures tend to keep a distance and not look directly at others when talking to them. People from both cultures can be **(2)** (adj.) congenial and sociable, but their communication styles vary depending on whether they were taught to assert themselves or **(3)** (v.) acquiesce.

Other animals also vary their communication **(4)** (n.) strategy, depending on the purpose and venue. For example, researchers at the University of St. Andrews have learned that monkeys in Nigeria have a language for warning each other. There is nothing **(5)** (adj.) equivocal about terms that indicate danger above or below or the need to flee. This is not an attempt to be **(6)** (adj.) manipulative and **(7)** (v.) wield power over other monkeys. It is an attempt to protect them.[1]

Similarly, ornithologists at the Max Planck Institutes in Germany have noticed that some male canaries are better singers and those songs are **(8)** (adj.) conducive to attracting the attention of female canaries who then have a **(9)** (n.) propensity for producing larger eggs if they hear the mating calls with complex ranges and "sexy syllables." Not only are the eggs larger, but the offspring seem to be healthier.[2]

Do you suppose that means humans will evolve physically as they enhance their vocabulary? The idea may **(10)** (v.) substantiate an argument for studying more words.

[1]Source: "Monkey Talk," *Smithsonian*, July 2006, p. 16

[2]Source: "An Etude for Egg Laying," *Smithsonian*, August 2006, p. 12.

Stop and Think

Using at least three words from the list, summarize the sociology passage in 50 words or less in the space below. (Answers will vary.)

Based on the ideas of Niccolo Machiavelli, the Mach scale reveals the role power plays in the lives of those surveyed and predicts whether people will be **manipulative** or **congenial** in their behavior and honest or **equivocal** in their responses. (40 words)

Write a caption for this picture using two of the words from the chapter.

Susan Pongratz

(Answers will vary.)

CHAPTER 19 Vocabulary in American Literature

Get Ready to Read About American Literature

Students sometimes register for a survey course in American literature to fulfill their major's humanities requirement. Such a course offers an overview of a variety of genres, or categories, in literature, including short stories, novels, essays, memoirs, plays, and poetry. The title of the following poem, "Javelina," is named after a variety of a hog found in the Southwest. The poet, Joy Harjo, is a Native American born in Tulsa, Oklahoma, and received her Master of Fine Arts from the University of New Mexico. Since then, she has taught at Arizona State University, Santa Fe Community College, and the Institute of American Indian Arts. Currently, she teaches at the University of California at Los Angeles.

Before you read, consider what you already know about the following word parts. The meanings of some have been provided. Recall what you learned in Chapter 1 and fill in the blanks for the others.

1. The prefix *pre-* means before ________.
2. The prefix *re-* means again ________.
3. The prefix *sub-* means under, below ________.
4. The suffix *-ance* means quality, state ________ and indicates a noun ________.
5. The suffix *-ly* means in the manner of ________ and usually indicates an adverb ________.
6. The suffix *-y* means *quality* or *trait* and often indicates a noun ________.

bristly	cicada	oracle	renascent	subtlety
chrysalis	forage	prevalent	renegade	sustenance

JAVELINA

by Joy Harjo

The sun falls onto the **bristly** backs of **foraging** javelina west of the desert **oracle,** and the soft streets stiffen with the crawling dark. I drive South Tucson. I am the one standing at a pay phone with a baby on her hip, just seventeen. Do I need a job? Has the car broken down again? Does the license plate say Oklahoma? I travel from a tribe whose name bears storm clouds, and have entered a land where a drink of water is a way to pray. I was born of a blood who wrestled the whites for freedom, and I have since lived dangerously in a diminished system. I, too, still forage as the sun goes down: for lava **sustenance.** The javelina knows what I mean. I can no longer imagine this poem without them, either their ghostly shapes of light-years reversed, or the tracks now skating behind them in the sand.

I want to stop the car and tell her she will find the way out of the soap opera. *The mythic world you enter with the* ***subtlety*** *of a snake the color of earth changing skin. Your wounded spirit is the* ***chrysalis*** *for a* ***renascent*** *butterfly. You son will graduate from high school. You have a daughter not yet born, and you who thought you could say nothing, write poetry.*

And would she believe me?
And does she now?

Her husband comes out of the cheap room with more change and a Coke. I cannot turn my head or lie; it has gotten me nowhere. I leave her there. But for years I pray for rain, for her beaten spirit to lift up and rain and rain. The **cicadas** enter with a song at the torn edge; they call forth the burning sunset the color of lips of the unseen guardian of mist. A **renegade** turtle hides beneath damp runners of a plant with red berries; tastes rain. I imagine the talk of pigs and hear them speak the coolest promise of spiny leaves. Their **prevalent** nightmare has entered recent genetic memory, as the smell of gun-powder mixed with human sweat.

I have done time on their streets, said an elder with thick tusks of wisdom. *And I have understood this desert without them. It is sweeter than the blooms of prickly pear. It is sweeter than rain.*

—"Javelina" by Joy Harjo from In Mad Love and War (Wesleyan University Press, 1990).

VISUAL VOCABULARY

Javelinas are a__________ in south Texas.

a. prevalent
b. bristly

Joe McDonald/Corbis

EXERCISE 1 Context Clues

Refer to the previous passage and use context clues from the sentences below to determine the definition of each of the following words in **bold** print. Do not consult a dictionary.

1. bristly (brĭs′lē) adj.
The angora sweater was soft but **bristly,** so Sara decided not to purchase it because comfort was her main concern.

__a__ **Bristly** means
a. rough. b. smooth. c. soft. d. comfortable.

2. chrysalis (krĭs′ə-lĭs) n.
The garden consisted only of milkweed in order to attract Monarch butterflies, and as a result, each plant had at least one **chrysalis** suspended like a pendant ready to open.

__c__ **Chrysalis** means
a. sparkle. b. moth. c. cocoon. d. butterfly.

3. cicada (sĭ-kā′də) n.
The North American species of **cicada** has an extremely long life cycle of 17 years, at which time they emerge and provide almost deafening keening during the "dog days" of summer in July and August.

__d__ **Cicada** means
a. transparent dragonfly.
b. sun flower.
c. delicate water lily.
d. stout insect with transparent wings.

4. forage (fôr′ĭj) v.
When the camp fire began to dwindle, we ventured out in pairs to **forage** for kindling.

__a__ **Forage** means
a. hunt. b. plant. c. deposit. d. cooperate.

5. oracle (ôr′ə-kəl) n.
Jamaica's grandmother had a sixth sense that earned her the reputation of family **oracle** because she had the ability to foresee danger in her dreams.

__a__ **Oracle** means
a. predictor. b. stalemate. c. explorer. d. gatherer.

6. prevalent (prĕv′ə-lənt) adj.
An unusual breed of white squirrels is as **prevalent** around the Biltmore Estate in Asheville, North Carolina, as the pigeons are in Central Park in New York City.

__b__ **Prevalent** means
a. rare. b. widespread. c. abnormal. d. common.

7. renascent (rĭ-năs′nət) adj.
From experience, Dan knew it would take some time after training and competing in the Boston Marathon before he felt **renascent** enough to think about going back to his job.

__c__ **Renascent** means
a. irritated. c. energetically renewed.
b. competed. d. exhausted.

8. renegade (rĕn′ĭ-gād) n.
Although his wardrobe was conventional, Tyson's nontraditional artwork caused some to consider him a **renegade.**

__a__ **Renegade** means
a. rebel. c. dull bore.
b. conservative. d. predictable person.

9. subtlety (sŭt′l-tē) n.
Showing no **subtlety** or compassion, the judge candidly asked the talent show hopeful if he had ever thought of selling CDs instead of trying to sing on one.

__b__ **Subtlety** means
a. harshness. b. diplomacy. c. toughness. d. innocence.

10. sustenance (sŭs′tə-nəns) n.
"A good meal is composed of food for **sustenance,** candles and flowers for atmosphere, and stimulating conversation for inspiration," explained the entertainment expert.

__c__ **Sustenance** means
a. expense. b. neglect. c. nourishment. d. obstacle.

EXERCISE 2 Word Sorts

Synonyms

Match the word to the synonyms or definitions that follow each blank.

1. cicada a large fly-like insect with transparent wings
2. oracle fortune teller; clairvoyant; seer; soothsayer
3. forage seek; hunt; search; pursue
4. sustenance food; fare; provision; edible
5. chrysalis pupa of a moth or butterfly protected in a firm case

Antonyms

Select the letter of the word(s) with the opposite meaning.

__d__ **6.** renascent
a. renewed c. reborn
b. revived d. dead

__a__ **7.** bristly
a. soft c. rough
b. harsh d. gravely

__a__ **8.** subtlety
a. straightforward c. daintiness
b. elegance d. complexity

__b__ **9.** prevalent
a. widespread c. common
b. rare d. present

__b__ **10.** renegade
a. defector c. traitor
b. conservative d. rebel

EXERCISE 3 Fill in the Blank

Use context clues to determine the word that best completes each sentence.

1. Each summer, just when the night-blooming cereus looks like it is dead, buds appear and its renascent __________ spirit reminds us that beauty is renewed in unexpected ways.
2. Although he was a renegade __________ as a youth, getting expelled from several schools, Paul Orfalea eventually found his stride as a businessman by creating Kinko's.
3. More prevalent __________ than they were 15 years ago, cell phones are becoming more sophisticated and someday they will serve as our credit cards and admittance into rock concerts.
4. The male cicada __________ has the ability to make one of the loudest sounds in the insect world by vibrating plates in its abdomen.
5. The butterfly kit we received came with the chrysalis __________ of a Painted Lady butterfly that emerged after only three weeks.
6. Many cultures have had oracle(s) __________ to help offer prophetic guidance.
7. For some, work is something to provide food on the table; for others, work provides another kind of sustenance __________: nourishment for their souls.
8. Her grandfather's bristly __________ beard always reminded Emma of rough sandpaper.
9. After several minutes of trying to forage __________ through her memory, Stacy decided on a topic discussed in class and settled down to begin her research.
10. The best time to fire a person is at 2:00 P.M. on a Friday afternoon, and it is appropriate to avoid compassion or subtlety __________ because a straightforward discussion is usually appreciated.

EXERCISE 4 Application

Using context clues, insert the vocabulary word in the appropriate blank. A part-of-speech clue is given for each vocabulary word.

Learning to write poetry is like learning to sculpt with words. You have an idea of what you want the poem to look like, and first you add layers, and then you chip away words. As you study the genre of poetry and try writing your own poems, you begin to notice that sometimes there are no rules.

Like the poet William Carlos Williams, a medical doctor who happened to write poetry about mundane things such as plums in the ice box or red wagons, you can write poems about the **(1)** (adj.) bristly spikes of a desert cactus ready to flower or the liberated keening of the **(2)** (n.) cicada(s) after lying dormant for 17 years or the promise of the **(3)** (n.) chrysalis about to release a butterfly.

Much of the intrigue of poetry is its **(4)** (n.) subtlety—what is left unsaid. All words count. For this reason, the poet **(5)** (v.) forages continually for subjects, words, images, and new ways to look at common things.

What may surprise you is that everyone is born with the eye of a child hungry for details, eager for answers. Poetry also supplies the human need for a **(6)** (adj.) renascent spirit—that longing that is universally **(7)** (adj.) prevalent, present in everyone, a way to be reborn. As a result, poets are often viewed as prophets, **(8)** (n.) oracle(s) of what is to come and as **(9)** (n.) renegade(s), rebelling against life as it exists and eager to journey a less-traveled path. The one thing all poets have in common is a hunger for words. Whether sailing alone around the room with poet Billy Collins or eating poetry with Mark Strand, we continue to travel through a tunnel of words, plough through the past, and attempt to make sense of the present. With poetry, we can find more than **(10)** (n.) sustenance; we find hope in things to come.

Stop and Think

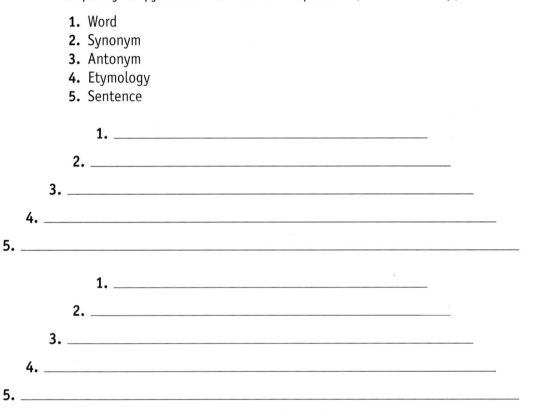

Pyramid Summary: Choose two words from this chapter and complete the pyramid summaries below. You may consult your dictionary or go to **www.dictionary.reference.com** and **www.etymonline.com** for additional help. Then compare your pyramids with those of a partner. (Answers will vary.)

1. Word
2. Synonym
3. Antonym
4. Etymology
5. Sentence

1. ______________________________
2. ________________________________
3. __________________________________
4. ____________________________________
5. ______________________________________

1. ______________________________
2. ________________________________
3. __________________________________
4. ____________________________________
5. ______________________________________

Go to the following site **http://www.cs.rice.edu/~ssiyer/minstrels/poems/676.html** to read Mark Strand's poem "Eating Poetry." On your own paper, write your ideas connected to the poem. (Answers will vary.)

CHAPTER 20

Vocabulary in World Literature

Get Ready to Read About World Literature

World literature is a course in humanities that explores a variety of themes and genres. In addition, students of world literature will also study the cultures and world history connected to their readings. This selection is a translation from the work of Jorge Luis Borges, an Argentine writer with an international reputation as a short story writer, poet, essayist, and critic.

Before you read, consider what you already know about the following word parts. The meanings of some have been provided. Recall what you learned in Chapter 1 and fill in the blanks for the others.

1. The prefix *con-* means with, together.
2. The prefix *pro-* means for, forward.
3. The root *ject* means throw.
4. The root *spec* means look, watch.
5. The suffix *-ate* means cause to become, make and usually indicates a verb.
6. The suffix *-ist* means person and indicates a noun.
7. The suffix *-ive* means *like, related to* and indicates an adjective.
8. The suffix *-tion* means *action, state* and indicates a noun.

appall	conjecture	imprecation	protagonist	suppress
confiscate	fathom	obscure	speculative	vestibule

FROM *PEDRO SALVADORES*

By Jorge Luis Borges

I want to put in writing, perhaps for the first time, one of the strangest and saddest events in the history of my country. The best way to go about it, I believe, is to keep my own part in the telling of the story small, and to **suppress** all picturesque additions and **speculative conjectures.**

A man, a woman, and the vast shadow of a dictator are the story's three **protagonists.** The man's name was Pedro Salvadores; my grandfather Acevedo was a witness to his existence, a few days or weeks after the Battle of Monte Caseros. There may have been no real difference between Pedro Salvadores and the common run of mankind, but his fate, the years of it, made him unique. He was a gentleman much like the other gentlemen of his day, with a place in the city and some land (we may imagine) in the country; he was a member of the Unitarian party. His wife's maiden name was Planes; they lived together on Calle Suipacha, not far from the corner of Temple. The house in which the events took place was much like the others on the street; the front door, the **vestibule,** the inner door, the rooms, the shadowy depth of the patios. One night in 1842, Pedro Salvadores and his wife heard the dull sound of hoofbeats coming closer and closer up the dusty street, and the wild huzzahs and **imprecations** of the horses' riders. But this time the horsemen of the tyrant's posse did not pass them by. The whooping and shouting became insistent banging on the door. Then, as the men were breaking down the door, Salvadores managed to push the dining table to one side, lift the rug, and hide himself in the cellar. His wife moved the table back into place. The posse burst into the house; they had come to get Salvadores. His wife told them he'd fled—to Montevideo, she told them. They didn't believe her; they lashed her with their whips, smashed all the sky blue china, and searched the house, but it never occurred to them to lift the rug. They left at midnight, vowing to return.

It is at this point that the story of Pedro Salvadores truly begins. He lived in that cellar for nine years. No matter how much we tell ourselves that years are made of days, and days of hours, and that nine years is an abstraction, an impossible sum, the story still horrifies and **appalls.** I suspect that in the darkness that his eyes learned to **fathom,** he came not to think of anything—not even his hatred or his danger. He was simply there, in the cellar. Now and again, echoes of that world he could not enter would reach him from above: his wife's footsteps as she went about her routine, the thump of the water pump and the pail, the pelting of rain in the patio. Every day, too, might be his last.

His wife gradually got rid of all the servants; they were capable of informing on him. She told her family that her husband was in Uruguay. She earned a living for the two of them by sewing for the army. In the course of time she had two children; her family attributing the children to a lover, repudiated her. After the fall of the tyrant, they got down on their knees and begged her forgiveness.

What, who, was Pedro Salvadores? Was he imprisoned by terror, love, the invisible presence of Buenos Aires, or, in the final analysis, habit? To keep him from leaving her, his wife would give him vague news of conspiracies and victories. Perhaps he was a coward, and his wife faithfully hid from him that she knew that. I picture him in his cellar, perhaps without even an oil lamp, or a book. The darkness would draw him under, into sleep. He would dream, at first, the dreadful night when the knife would seek the throat, or dream of open streets, or of the plains. Within a few years he would be incapable of fleeing, and he would dream of the cellar. At first he was a hunted man, a man in danger; later . . . we will never know—a quiet animal in its burrows or some sort of **obscure** deity?

All this until that summer day in 1852 when the dictator Rosas fled the country. It was then that the secret man emerged into the light of day; my grandfather actually spoke with him. Puffy, slack-muscled, and obese, Pedro Salvadores was the color of wax, and he spoke in a faint whisper. The government had **confiscated** his land; it was never returned to him. I believe he died in poverty.

We see the fate of Pedro Salvadores, like all things, as a symbol of something that we are just on the verge of understanding.

VISUAL VOCABULARY

Because of the undergrowth and numerous trees, paths in deep woods are often b__________ from a distance.

a. speculative
b. obscure

Elizabeth Pongratz

EXERCISE 1 Context Clues

Refer to the previous passage and use context clues from the sentences below to determine the definition of each of the following words in **bold** print. Do not consult a dictionary.

1. appall (ə-pôl′) v.
Nina was usually shy and reserved, so her outspoken, impolite behavior during the wedding reception **appalled** the guests.

__d__ **Appall** means
a. surround. b. appeal to. c. please. d. shock.

2. confiscate (kŏn′fĭ-skāt′) v.
Debra parked in a no parking zone for the fifth time, so the campus police towed and impounded her car, later explaining that they **confiscated** her vehicle because she had been a repeat offender.

__c__ **Confiscate** means
a. reveal. c. take possession of.
b. accept. d. restore.

3. conjecture (kən-jĕk′chər) n.
The chemistry study group agreed that anticipating the exam questions involved **conjecture,** but making a practice test was still a good strategy.

__a__ **Conjecture** means
a. guess. b. reason. c. method. d. sport.

4. fathom (făth′əm) v.
Even with some prior knowledge of Spanish, Joseph admitted he could not **fathom** some of the questions on the essay portion of the test.

__b__ **Fathom** means
a. question. c. misunderstand.
b. figure out. d. teach.

5. imprecation (ĭm′prĭ-kā′shən) n.
After drifting at sea in the lifeboat for three days, the survivors no longer angrily spewed **imprecations** at each other; instead, they began to consider what was needed to stay alive.

__a__ **Imprecation** means
a. curse. c. water.
b. compliment. d. praise.

6. obscure (ob-skyo͞or′) adj.
Professor Wiseman's instructions for the project were so **obscure** that we decided to email him for clarification.

__b__ **Obscure** means
a. clear. b. unclear. c. well known. d. obvious.

7. protagonist (prō-tăg′ə-nĭst) n.
The **protagonist** of the story was a bespectacled orphan, hardly the type you would expect to be a hero.

__c__ **Protagonist** means
a. author. c. central character.
b. foil. d. sidekick.

8. speculative (spĕk′yə-lə-tĭv) adj.
The **speculative** nature of the business venture seemed too risky since there were no assurances that it would work.

__a__ **Speculative** means
a. indefinite; imagined. c. definite; practical.
b. sensible; reasonable. d. reliable; loyal.

9. suppress (sə-prĕs′) v.
The government press release was not completely honest because it **suppressed** information the public needed to know to understand the full truth.

__a__ **Suppress** means
a. hold back. b. release. c. express. d. submit.

10. vestibule (vĕs′tə-byo͞ol′) n.
From the receptionist's desk in the **vestibule** of the administration building, Cindy was able to see anyone entering and exiting the area.

__c__ **Vestibule** means
a. basement. b. elevator. c. entrance hall. d. roof.

EXERCISE 2 Word Sorts

Synonyms

Match the word to the synonyms or definitions that follow each blank.

1. __protagonist__ hero; lead; star; principal
2. __imprecation__ curse; malediction; denunciation; anathema

3. speculative theoretical; risky; uncertain; characterized by guessing

4. appall shock; dismay; horrify

5. vestibule portal; anteroom; foyer; entryway

Antonyms

Select the letter of the word(s) with the opposite meaning.

b 6. suppress
a. cover up
b. reveal
c. muffle
d. receive

a 7. conjecture
a. conclusion
b. guess
c. lesson
d. prediction

d 8. fathom
a. comprehend
b. forgive
c. wonder
d. misunderstand

c 9. obscure
a. circular
b. neat
c. clear
d. vague

b 10. confiscate
a. seize
b. donate
c. resist
d. insist

EXERCISE 3 Fill in the Blank

Use context clues to determine the word that best completes each sentence.

1. We repeatedly read the poem trying to untangle the meaning of each line and fathom the poet's theme.

2. In *Romeo and Juliet,* Mercutio is fatally stabbed and shouts the imprecation, "A plague o' both your houses!"

3. Looking over the obscure instructions, Tori realized she needed to talk with the client to prevent miscommunication on the project.

4. We waited in the vestibule of the hotel until the storm subsided before we ventured out to the city.

5. According to the syllabus, the professor will confiscate cell phones that ring in class.

6. Although investing in the stock was purely speculative, the decision was a good one despite the uncertainty and risk involved.

7. Sarai had to suppress her laughter when her professor entered with a carelessly buttoned shirt and mismatched shoes.

8. During the curtain call at the end of the play, the protagonist drew cheers from the audience because everyone loves a hero; however, the appearance of the evil villain prompted a standing ovation because of his excellent performance.

9. Emma was appall(ed) when she learned the Department of Agriculture and city officials had rounded up families of Canada geese and transported them to a meat packing plant.

10. During the interview, Kristin studied the applicant and made the conjecture that she was a congenial woman who would be willing to learn the job and work hard to help the company.

EXERCISE 4 Application

Using context clues, insert the vocabulary word in the appropriate blank. A part-of-speech clue is given for each vocabulary word.

Cassie entered the front door of the home of her boyfriend's parents. On a table in the **(1)** (n.) vestibule rose a stack of books, some by authors she had been studying in her college English class, others by **(2)** (adj.) obscure writers she did not know. Trying to **(3)** (v.) suppress her feeling of anxiety, Cassie took a deep breath. She wanted to make a good impression, but her **(4)** (adj.) speculative nature tended to prompt the worst images of her imagination. Here she was meeting famous scholars, and she suddenly could not **(5)** (v.) fathom what she would have in common with these brilliant, erudite people. Not only that, they were two of the wealthiest people in the country.

How can I sustain a conversation without making them **(6)** (v.) appalled ______ *at their son's choice in women?* she wondered.

Cassie was not a rich woman. She had not traveled to Europe. She did not know how to play golf or tennis or bridge. She sighed. *Will they think I'm a pseudo-intellectual?* Suddenly she felt like the **(7)** (n.) protagonist ______ of the Jane Austen novel *Pride and Prejudice.*

Todd squeezed her hand in reassurance as they entered the living room. "They will love you," he promised.

Cassie gave a tentative smile and took a deep breath. She felt like an interloper, an intruder here to **(8)** (v.) confiscate ______ the family silver. *What are you afraid of? Do you think they will escort you out with the* **(9)** (n.) imprecation(s) ______ *of an angry couple trying to protect their family?*

But Todd was right. She had nothing to fear.

If they had shared any negative **(10)** (n.) conjecture ______ about their son's choice in a girlfriend, their fears were quickly eliminated when they met Cassie—especially when they discovered a common interest in literature of the Regency period.

Stop and Think

Reread the passage from *Pedro Salvadores* and then, using two vocabulary words, summarize the selection in 60 words or less. (Answers may vary; a sample is provided.)

The **protagonist** of Borges's story hid in his basement while his land was confiscated and his wife fielded **conjectures** and **imprecations** about her virtue. Eventually when he emerged from his sanctuary, Pedro appeared as the shell of a man with a life unlived, prompting the **appalled** reader to wonder if playing it safe is the coward's way. (57 words)

Select three words from the chapter. Write a synonym for each, and then draw a picture to connect to the word. (Answers will vary.)

Word	Synonym	Image
1.		
2.		
3.		

CHAPTER

21 Vocabulary in Art History

Get Ready to Read About Art History

Art history is a humanities course that presents information about a variety of art genres as they relate to a culture and the events of a particular time period.

Before you read, consider what you already know about the following word parts. Recall what you learned in Chapter 1 and fill in the blanks.

1. The prefix *re-* means again.
2. The suffix *-ate* means cause to become, make and indicates a verb.

elicit	fissure	montage	radiate	rite
essence	grandeur	quarry	replica	sanctuary

CAVE PAINTING

The Cave of Lascaux (lahs-KOH) in France lies slightly over a mile from the little town of Montignac, in the valley of Vézère (vay-Zair) River. The cave itself was discovered in 1940 by a group of children who, while investigating a tree uprooted by a storm, scrambled down a **fissure** into a world undisturbed for thousands of years. The cave was sealed in 1963 to protect it from atmospheric damage, and visitors now see Lascaux II, an exact **replica,** which is sited in a **quarry** 600 feet away.

Perhaps a **sanctuary** for the performance of sacred **rites** and ceremonies, the Main Hall, or Hall of the Bulls, **elicits** a sense of power and

grandeur. The thundering herd moves below a sky formed by the rolling contours of the stone ceiling of the cave, sweeping our eyes forward as we travel into the cave itself. At the entrance of the main hall, the 8-foot "unicorn" begins a larger-than-lifesize **montage** of bulls, horses, and deer, which are up to 12 feet tall. Their shapes intermingle with one another, and their colors **radiate** warmth and power. These magnificent creatures remind us that their creators were capable technicians, who, with artistic skills at least equal to our own, were able to capture the **essence** beneath the visible surface of their world. The paintings in the Main Hall were created over a long period of time and by a succession of artists. Yet their cumulative effect in this 30- by 100-foot domed gallery is that of a single work, carefully composed for maximum dramatic and communicative impact.

—Adapted from Sporre, *The Creative Impulse,* 6th ed., pp. 41–43. Prentice Hall. Reprinted with permission.

VISUAL VOCABULARY

Palm trees a_____________ feelings of freedom and carefree thoughts.

a. elicit
b. radiate

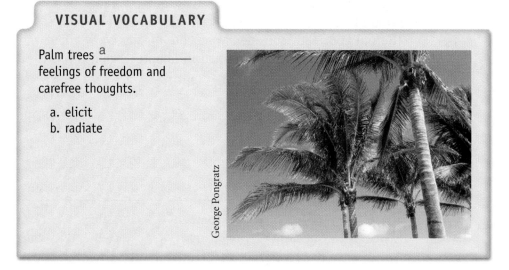

George Pongratz

EXERCISE 1 Context Clues

Refer to the previous passage and use context clues from the sentences below to determine the definition of each of the following words in **bold** print. Do not consult a dictionary.

1. elicit (ĭ-lĭs′ĭt) v.
When Dr. Sykes jokingly referred to Annie as the "man in black" because of her dark clothes, she managed to **elicit** some laughter when she said in a deep, gravely voice, "Hello, my name is Johnny Cash."

__a__ **Elicit** means
a. draw out. b. suppress c. hide. d. surface.

2. essence (ĕs′əns) n.
Writer Eudora Welty once said that if the **essence** of a story could be expressed in one sentence then it was not a real story.

__b__ **Essence** means
a. detail b. core. c. topic. d. exterior.

3. fissure (fĭsh′ər) n.
A few minutes after the earthquake, we discovered a **fissure** gaping in the middle of the highway.

__a__ **Fissure** means
a. fracture. b. closure. c. mountain. d. bulge.

4. grandeur (grăn′jər) n.
Architects have designed a glass-enclosed walkway that juts over a cliff in the Grand Canyon so people will be able to view the **grandeur** of nature from a lofty angle.

__a__ **Grandeur** means
a. splendor. b. obscurity. c. rock. d. lowliness.

5. montage (mŏn-täzh′) n.
PhotoStory 3 is a free software program that allows you to display a **montage** of pictures with accompanying music.

__b__ **Montage** means
a. transition. b. assortment. c. topic. d. thesis.

6. quarry (kwôr′ē) n.
The sculptor went to the rock **quarry** and chose a beautiful piece of marble for his next project.

__d__ **Quarry** means
a. owner. b. museum. c. hunter. d. pit.

7. radiate (rā′dē-āt′) v.
Although she was a stranger, she seemed to **radiate** an innate kindness and a personal magnetism that generated trust among everyone.

__a__ **Radiate** means
a. give off; exude.
b. darken; dull.
c. dim.
d. absorb; saturate.

8. replica (rĕp′lĭ-kə) n.
Even though the original fort no longer exists, a **replica** was built as a museum so that visitors could experience life in the West.

___c___ **Replica** means
a. rebound. b. genuine article. c. duplicate. d. original.

9. rite (rīt) n.
As a **rite** to instill personal confidence, some people learn "mind over matter" by walking barefoot across hot coals.

___c___ **Rite** means
a. obligation.
b. informality.
c. tradition; act of initiation.
d. freedom; legal right.

10. sanctuary (săngk′cho͞o-ĕr′ē) n.
Through visual imagery, Wade created a personal mental **sanctuary,** consisting of smooth boulders overlooking an ocean in an isolated, yet very safe, area.

___b___ **Sanctuary** means
a. exposure. b. safe place. c. silence. d. abandonment.

EXERCISE 2 Word Sorts

Synonyms

Match the word to the synonyms or definitions that follow each blank.

1. ___rite___ ritual; tradition; celebration; ordeal

2. ___fissure___ crack; crevasse; cleft; crevice

3. ___radiate___ exude; glow; beam; spread out in rays

4. ___quarry___ a place where building stone, marble, or slate is excavated

5. ___montage___ collage; panorama; composition; collection of several pictures

Antonyms

Select the letter of the word(s) with the opposite meaning.

___c___ **6.** sanctuary
a. haven
b. large room
c. dangerous place
d. safe place

___d___ **7.** essence
a. core b. heart c. memory d. detail

a **8.** replica
a. original b. duplicate c. copy d. plan

b **9.** elicit
a. measure b. instill c. exit d. draw out

c **10.** grandeur
a. splendor
b. friendly
c. disappointment
d. magnificence

EXERCISE 3 Fill in the Blank

Use context clues to determine the word that best completes each sentence.

1. The city established a bird sanctuary by the lake, and it became a safe place for the swans and Canada geese.
2. The grandeur of the Redwood Forest is difficult to imagine and must be seen in person to experience its magnificence.
3. Bill Fox, a naval architect, likes to create tiny replicas of sailing ships inside bottles.
4. Sociologists recognize a rite of passage in a culture as an important milestone or tradition, particularly indicating a coming-of-age event such as a first haircut or getting a driver's license.
5. Josh began the eulogy to celebrate his mother's life with a comment to elicit surprised laughter and ease tension by saying, "My father didn't die twenty years ago; he escaped."
6. Their broken relationship had become a fissure, a chasm, a gorge across which they would have to throw a fragile ladder and begin to cross wrung by wrung.
7. Her husband never reads books, only the reviews of books, thinking if he knows the essence of the story, then he can appear well read.
8. Heat radiate(d) from the sidewalk, creating the optical illusion of distant pools of water.
9. A favorite swimming area was the old rock quarry, but people were cautioned not to swim alone since water levels were dangerously deep.

10. Reading the old letters prompted a montage________ of memories—for him, it was like flipping through a Master ViewFinder and seeing a series of pictures.

EXERCISE 4 Application

Using context clues, insert the vocabulary word in the appropriate blank. A part-of-speech clue is given for each vocabulary word.

In planning the itinerary during her study abroad experience in France, Michelle went to **www.greatbuildings.com** to determine some architecture she wanted to see. One site showed a **(1)** (n.) montage________ of pictures of Chartres Cathedral, a structure that has **(2)** (v.) elicit(ed)________ the admiration and awe of builders since before the 13th century.

The **(3)** (n.) essence________ of gothic architecture, the cathedral is well-known for its **(4)** (n.) grandeur________ and beauty. It was a place of religious **(5)** (n.) rite(s)________ such as weddings, baptisms, funerals, and daily mass. It was also a functional building since it was a site for the social activity of the area. A masonry structure, the cathedral was constructed of stone hauled by volunteers from a local **(6)** (n.) quarry________ five miles away.

The cathedral was built and rebuilt over a period of 200 years having been destroyed in parts by fire and a lightning strike that left a huge **(7)** (n.) fissure________ between the west towers and the crypt.

Although the parishioners at first despaired over the destruction of their church, they were soon heartened by what they called a miracle when they discovered their sacred relic, the *Sancta Camisia,* had been spared. Work to rebuild the cathedral ensued.

Today the **(8)** (n.) sanctuary________ is the site of a famous labyrinth that visitors walk as well as impressive stained glass that **(9)** (v.) radiate(s)________ with light. The building also continues to inspire architects, but no **(10)** (n.) replica could ever duplicate the magnificence the structure exudes.

—Source: http://en.wikipedia.org/wiki/Cathedral_of_Chartres

Stop and Think

Using at least three words from the list, summarize the passage in 50 words or less in the space below. (Answers will vary; a sample is given.)

Cave paintings found near a **quarry** in France have **elicited** fascination of tourists and historians and confirm that the **essence** of all people's desire to communicate is part of their need to create. (33 words)

Study the pictures below and decide which vocabulary word from this chapter best summarizes the image. Write the word, the definition, and your reason for choosing the word. (Answers may vary.)

Courtesy of Microsoft.	1. fissure	The crack in the picture is an example of a fissure.
Courtesy of Microsoft.	2. montage	This collection of pictures is an example of a montage of images.
Courtesy of Microsoft.	3. radiate	The sun radiates light and heat as is indicated by the rays.
Courtesy of Microsoft.	4. replica	This toy is a replica of a real life airplane.

CHAPTER

22 Vocabulary in Philosophy

Get Ready to Read About Philosophy

A survey course in philosophy will introduce ideas that elicit reflective and insightful discussions about fundamental knowledge, what makes something right or wrong, the value and measure of truth, beauty, and reality. The word *philosophy* comes from the Greek roots *phil* (love) and *soph* (wisdom). The methods used in a philosophy course often involve the ability to reason, to evaluate, and to support arguments. The excerpt you are about to read is about a Chinese school of thought that is also sometimes referred to as Chinese religious movement.

Before you read, consider what you already know about the following word parts. The meanings of some have been provided. Recall what you learned in Chapter 1 and fill in the blanks for the others.

1. The prefix *con-* means with, together.
2. The prefix *pro-* means for, forward.
3. The root *cryp* means secret, hidden.
4. The root *cor* means heart.
5. The suffix *-ance* means quality, state and usually indicates a noun.

accordance	conviction	divine	profound	vigor
barren	cryptic	entwinement	rudimentary	void

TAOISM

Of Chinese origin, Taoism (DOW-ism) can be traced to the writings of Lao-tzu, who is believed to have lived some time during the 6th century B.C.E., but about whom little else is known. Lao-tzu simply means "the old one" and may be purely legendary. The book attributed to "the old one," known as the *Tao Te Ching* (Dow De Jing) or *The Way of Life* and reprinted continually, is a slender volume of short poems, often **cryptic,** seemingly simple but at the same time extremely **profound,** containing the view that the Way is an important **divine** order that rules the universe. Taoism is a religion only in the sense that its followers are obligated to live their lives in **accordance** with this order.

Rudimentary to Taoism is the **conviction** that the Tao operates through the continual interactions of opposites: joy and pain, for example, birth and death, male and female, day and night, cold and heat, success and failure. We cannot embrace life without being prepared for death. The fear of death—or, for that matter, of any thing opposite to what we hold dear—leads to suffering. If youth, **vigor,** and unwrinkled good looks are of vital importance, we must know that they cannot last and must therefore feel no anguish with the oncoming of age. Success and failure are implicit in the way the world goes. Today's failure might be tomorrow's brilliant achiever.

The universe was created by **entwinement** of the fundamental opposites: yin, the passive element, and yang, the active energy. In Chinese art, yin and yang are visually represented as a circle with a white crescent and a black crescent, each side containing a smaller circle, which has the other's color. The white crescent, yang, is the sun, the source of all life, and is traditionally known as the masculine principle; the black crescent, yin, is the moon, the passive and, traditionally, the feminine principle. The passive yin requires the driving force of the active yang to bring forth the variety of things that go to make up the world. The two are equal partners. Without yin, the universe is cold and lifeless, a **barren void.** Without yang, yin cannot create.

—Adapted from Janaro and Altshuler, *The Art of Being Human,* pp. 417–18.
Reprinted with permission.

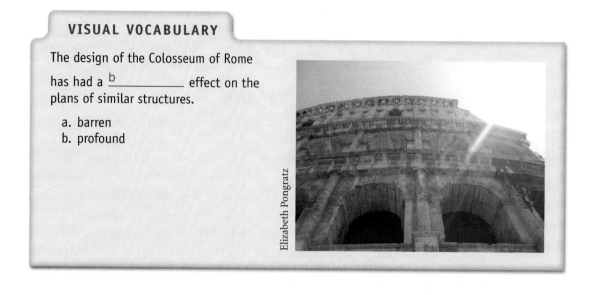

VISUAL VOCABULARY

The design of the Colosseum of Rome has had a b__________ effect on the plans of similar structures.

a. barren
b. profound

Elizabeth Pongratz

EXERCISE 1 Context Clues

Refer to the previous passage and use context clues from the sentences below to determine the definition of each of the following words in **bold** print. Do not consult a dictionary.

1. accordance (ə-kôr′dns) n.
In **accordance** with the contract, the co-owner agreed to offer to sell his shares of the company to his partner before considering other buyers' offers.

__a__ **Accordance** means
a. agreement. b. conflict. c. discussion. d. disagreement.

2. barren (băr′ən) adj.
The desert may look **barren** and devoid of any life at first glance, but it is actually full of life and at times it even blooms with a variety of flowers.

__b__ **Barren** means
a. fertile. b. unproductive. c. hospitable. d. alive.

3. conviction (kən-vĭk′shən) n.
Emil debated the issue with such **conviction** and passion that even his professor seemed ready to change his opinion based on his confident argument.

__d__ **Conviction** means
a. fear. b. guilt. c. doubt. d. confidence.

4. cryptic (krĭp′tĭk) adj.
Jason cringed as he read the note and admitted that there was nothing **cryptic** about the words, "We need to talk."

__d__ **Cryptic** means
a. comforting.
b. honest.
c. straightforward.
d. mysterious.

5. divine (dĭ-vīn′) adj.
Some people spend their lives seeking logical explanations, whereas others look for evidence of **divine** intervention and proof of angels.

__c__ **Divine** means
a. lifeless. b. disappointing. c. heavenly. d. evil.

6. entwinement (ĕn-twīn′mĕnt) n.
The rapid **entwinement** of kudzu vines and hydrangeas created a mass of green tangles impossible to unravel.

__d__ **Entwinement** means
a. growth.
b. unraveling.
c. separation.
d. twisting together.

7. profound (prə-found′) adj.
"One of the most **profound** ideas I learned in college," explained Tom, a civil engineer, "was from a British writer named Ben Brunwin who said, 'Good talk precedes good writing.'"

__a__ **Profound** means
a. insightful. b. meaningless. c. superficial. d. worthless.

8. rudimentary (rōō′də-mĕn′tə-rē) adj.
To follow even **rudimentary** cooking instructions, you must build a vocabulary that includes words such as *baste, broil, fold,* and *sear.*

__b__ **Rudimentary** means
a. sophisticated.
b. basic.
c. complex.
d. flavorful.

9. vigor (vĭg′ər) n.
"**Vigor** and energy are tied to one's attitude about life and work," explained the motivational speaker.

__b__ **Vigor** means
a. sluggishness. b. vitality. c. inactivity. d. success.

10. void (void) n.
Following her break-up, Nicole first slipped into a **void,** an emotional hole, but after some time, she shed her sadness and drew strength from the past.

__a__ **Void** means
a. emptiness. b. vacation. c. job. d. trip.

EXERCISE 2 Word Sorts

Synonyms

Match the word to the synonyms or definitions that follow each blank.

1. cryptic ____ secret; hidden; puzzling; enigmatic
2. entwinement ____ weaving together
3. divine ____ religious; sacrosanct; holy; sacred
4. conviction ____ confidence; certainty; assurance; passion
5. void ____ hollowness; emptiness; abyss; nothingness

Antonyms

Select the letter of the word(s) with the opposite meaning.

__c__ **6.** rudimentary
a. basic c. advanced
b. fundamental d. simple

__b__ **7.** accordance
a. agreement c. purpose
b. disagreement d. cooperation

__a__ **8.** profound
a. shallow c. tender
b. deep d. remarkable

__d__ **9.** barren
a. lifeless c. colorless
b. dull d. alive

__b__ **10.** vigor
a. color c. energy
b. exhaustion d. liveliness

EXERCISE 3 Fill in the Blank

Use context clues to determine the word that best completes each sentence.

1. Learning the rudimentary__________ basics of algebra are necessary before you can move to calculus.
2. In accordance__________ with the lease, Sara had to continue to make monthly payments on her apartment after the spring semester ended.
3. Dana left this cryptic__________ note on her boyfriend's windshield: "You are an expert kite flyer on a blustery day—someone who will always give me plenty of lead but never let go of the string."
4. Instead of looking exhausted, Barb was the picture of vigor__________ even after participating in the 5K fundraiser race.
5. Seeing the documentary had such a profound__________ effect on Trey that he changed his major to meteorology, hoping to find ways to deal with global warming.
6. With some new irrigation techniques, the farmland was no longer barren__________ but beginning to show new life.
7. The florist arranged an entwinement__________ of ribbons and ivy around tall candle holders for the night wedding.
8. Listening to the lecture, René felt unprepared and drifted into a mental void__________, unable to pick up a comprehensible thread in the presentation.
9. Amanda taught the group several strategies for using new technology with such conviction__________ that even the seasoned teachers agreed to try it in their classrooms.
10. After attending the student symphony, Sara wrote a review for the campus newspaper that said, "This was the closest I have been to the divine__________, just one note short of heaven."

EXERCISE 4 Application

Using context clues, insert the vocabulary word in the appropriate blank. A part-of-speech clue is given for each vocabulary word.

"Good stories and movies are circles with endings that have closure relating to the beginning," explained Katy as she talked about her essay to her writing group.

In **(1)** (n.) accordance ______ with the theory of a writing group, the four students used active listening skills to guide each other as they pondered their topics and the way they planned to expand them. Together, as a study group, they had reviewed the **(2)** (adj.) rudimentary ______ rules of grammar and always offered editing tips about ways to make a sentence sound better or how to fix a fragment or a comma splice. Today, however, they were the sounding board for Katy as she talked through the ideas she hoped to incorporate in her paper.

"I like your idea, Katy. In fact, it could be insightful and **(3)** (adj.) profound ______," Rosa said. "How do you propose to develop it?"

"Well, I thought I'd use some examples from movies and literature that show the circle."

"You mean like the flashback and the feather in *Forrest Gump*?" asked Melissa.

"Exactly. And even the black-and-white scenes in *The Wizard of Oz*?" added Annie.

"Another good one," said Jane. "But how about something from literature that is considered great but does not work with the circle. It would be good to show you have also considered those pieces in your paper."

"Oh, you mean like *Faust*?" asked Katy.

"Faust is a good choice," added Rosa. "He sells his soul at the beginning, then meets the beautiful woman who represents the **(4)** (n.) divine ______ spirit in all of us. Their emotional **(5)** (n.) entwinement ______ is tender. But then she dies and goes to heaven, and he has to be separated from her and lives in a spiritual **(6)** (n.) void__________. For him, nothing is gained."

"In that case, the readers gain, though, if they learn from Faust's mistake," added Melissa with the **(7)** (n.) conviction__________ of an avid reader bent on using words and ideas to enhance her life. "There is no **(8)** (adj.) cryptic__________ or mysterious message about learning from past errors of others—especially in great literature."

"Good idea. I'll include that as well," said Katy. "Thanks for your help. At least my well of ideas is no longer **(9)** (adj.) barren__________. In fact, this whole session has been very productive!" she added with more enthusiasm and **(10)** (n.) vigor__________ than when she began.

"Great!" exclaimed Rosa. "Now, let's talk about my research on Descartes," she said smiling.

Stop and Think

Use a highlighter to color in the circles next to the words you can define without looking at the definitions, and then pair up with a classmate to share your answers.

○ barren ○ accordance ○ entwinement

○ profound ○ conviction ○ cryptic ○ void

○ vigor ○ divine ○ rudimentary

Go to **www.etymonline.com** to study the history of the following words. Then complete the summaries by filling in the blanks.

1. cryptic

   In 1432, the word meant "cavern or grotto" from the Latin word for vault, which originated from the Greek, meaning "hidden." In 1789, it was used to indicate an underground burial area of a church. The prefix *crypto-* means secret and has been the meaning since 1760.

2. rudimentary

   The word rudimentary appeared in 1839, but first appeared in 1548 from Middle French and meant *early training, first experience, beginning, first principle.* The Latin word *rudis* means unlearned, untrained.

3. vigor

   Around 1300, *vigour* meant active, lively and originated from the Latin *vigorem* and *vigere.*

4. void

   Around 1290 the word meant "unoccupied, vacant" and originated from the Latin words *vocivus* and *vacuus* meaning empty. Around 1300, it was used as a verb to mean to clear. By 1420, the word was used to mean "lacking" or "wanting." By 1433, it indicated something legally invalid. In 1727, it was used as a noun to mean empty space, vacuum.

UNIT 5

5

Review Test
Chapters 18–22

1 Word Parts

A. Match the definitions in Column 2 to the word parts in Column 1.

Column 1	Column 2
j **1.** equ	a. for; forward
i **2.** gen	b. look; watch
e **3.** -ly	c. heart
h **4.** ject	d. hidden; secret
c **5.** cor	e. in the manner of
f **6.** -ance	f. quality; state
g **7.** -al	g. of, like, related to
b **8.** spec	h. throw
d **9.** crypt	i. birth; kindred
a **10.** pro	j. equal

2 Fill in the Blank

Use context clues to determine the best word from the box to complete each sentence.

acquiesce	bristly	imprecation	montage	rite
barren	essence	manipulative	oracle	void

5

1. The poet's prophetic words foretold visions as accurately as a(n) oracle ________ of Greek times warned the citizens of the future.

2. Leaving home at 23 after graduation from college and getting his own apartment was a rite ________ of passage for Sam—a tradition that his brothers had established.

3. The essence ________ of the play was that life is mystical and mystifying.

4. Chris looked at his life as a void ________, without purpose or substance, until he traveled to New Zealand and discovered his niche.

5. Having learned to assert herself, Matty offered help to a new co-worker who always felt the need to acquiesce ________ rather than express her ideas.

6. A manipulative ________ supervisor uses tactics that make employees fearful and distrustful.

7. The classic film *The Great Escape* is an exciting adventure based on a true story of World War II POWs who try to flee the prison camp, and one surprise is that there is not one imprecation ________ or offensive phrase in the entire movie.

8. The barren ________ land showed little promise of cultivation, but with irrigation and proper planning, the Afghan farmers are hopeful for a good harvest of apricots and almonds.

9. To protect herself from the bristly ________ underbrush as she cleared the ranch, Gabrielle wore long sleeves and work gloves.

10. The memories of his summer romance played like a photographic montage ________, and already he dreaded fall and the new semester.

3 Book Connection

Use context clues to determine the best word from the box to complete each sentence. A part of speech clue is provided for each vocabulary word.

divine	fissure	grandeur	strategy	sustenance
elicit	forage	propensity	suppress	vigor

BETWEEN A ROCK AND A HARD PLACE

Aaron Ralston was a 27-year-old who was an experienced climber when he ventured out one day on his own. Full of **(1)** (n.) vigor ________ and enthusiasm for the **(2)** (n.) grandeur ________ of the Utah mountains, he did not tell anyone where he was going because he anticipated no problem.

But a problem did arise during his climb. Wedged in a **(3)** (n.) fissure ________ of the mountain was an 800-pound boulder that broke loose and pinned Ralston so that he was unable to break free. Five days later, with little **(4)** (n.) sustenance ________ and his ration of water disappearing, Ralston **(5)** (v.) suppress(ed) ________ his fear, summoned his courage, and made a life-changing decision. His **(6)** (n.) strategy ________? His plan involved using a tourniquet and amputating his arm.

Ralston's story, *Between a Rock and a Hard Place,* is an autobiography that **(7)** (v.) elicit(s) ________ the amazement and admiration of readers who say this event was a true test of courage. Whether readers interpret his story as a sign of **(8)** (adj.) divine ________ intervention or the pragmatic critical thinking of a man who rises to the level of hero, the story is a riveting one, although the graphic description of the amputation may not be for the faint of heart.

Ralston has a **(9)** (n.) propensity ________ for adventure. Prior to that fateful day, he almost died after being buried for 15 minutes in an avalanche. And since that day, he continues to **(10)** (v.) forage ________ for new quests laced with similar dangers.

4 Visual Connection

Write a caption for this picture using two of the words from the box.

cicada	obscure	quarry	replica	sanctuary
conviction	profound	radiate	rudimentary	vestibule

5

George Pongratz

(Answers will vary.)

5 Analogies

Choose the word that best completes the analogy.

1. pledge : initiation :: freshman : ___a___
   a. orientation b. propensity c. sustenance
2. details : support :: evidence : ___c___
   a. acquiesce b. wield c. substantiate
3. money : spend :: power : ___a___
   a. wield b. substantiate c. appall
4. womb : baby :: cocoon : ___a___
   a. chrysalis b. conjecture c. renegade
5. scarce : plentiful :: rare : ___c___
   a. renascent b. subtlety c. prevalent
6. supporter : rebel :: advocate : ___b___
   a. conjecture b. renegade c. sustenance
7. comment : tact :: humor : ___c___
   a. orientation b. protagonist c. subtlety
8. delight : surprise :: shock : ___a___
   a. appall b. suppress c. substantiate
9. contribution : donate :: property : ___a___
   a. confiscate b. wield c. acquiesce
10. misunderstand : misinterpret :: understand : ___b___
    a. radiate b. fathom c. appall

APPENDIX A

Word Parts

Roots

Root	Meaning	Example
alter	change	altercation
ama	love	amorous
anima	breath, spirit	animated
anno	year	annual
aqua	water	aquifer
aster, astro	star	asteroid
aud	hear	auditory
bene	good	beneficial
bio	life	biology
cap	head	decapitate
cap, capt	take	captivate
card, cor, cord	heart	cardiologist, core
ced, ceed, cess	go	proceed
cosmo	order, universe	cosmos
cresc	grow, increase	crescendo
cryp	secret, hidden	crypt
dent	tooth	dentist
derm	skin	epidermis
dict	say	predict
duc, duct	lead, guide	conductor
dynam	power	dynamic
ego	self	egotistical
equ, equal	equal	equilibrium
err, errat	wander	erratic
ethno	race, tribe	ethnic
fac, fact	do, make	factory
fer	carry	transfer
flu, fluct, flux	flow	influx
fract	break	fracture
frater	brother	fraternal
gene	race, kind, sex	genetics

Root	Meaning	Example
grad, gres	go, take, steps	graduate
graph	write, draw	autograph
gyn	woman	gynecologist
hab, habi	have, hold	habitat
hap	change	happenstance
helio	sun, light	heliograph
ject	throw	eject
lat	carry	translate
lic, liqu, list	leave behind	liquidate
lith	stone	monolith
loc	place	relocate
log	speech, science, reason	logic
loquor	speak	colloquial
lumen, lumin	light	luminary
macro	large	macroeconomics
manu	hand	manual
mater	mother	maternal
med	middle	mediator
meter	measure	thermometer
micro	small	microorganism
miss, mit	send, let go	transmit
morph	form	morpheme
mort	die	mortal
mot, mov	movement	demote
mut, muta	change	mutation
nat	be born	natural, native
neg, negat	say no, deny	negate, negative
nomen, nym	name	antonym, synonym
pel, puls	push, drive	propel
philo	love	philanthropy
ocul	eye	monocle
ortho	right, straight	orthodontist
osteo	bone	osteoporosis
pater	father	paternal
path	suffering, feeling	pathology
ped	child	pediatrician
ped, pod	foot	podiatrist
phobia	fear	claustrophobia
phon	sound	telephone
photo	light	photograph
plic	fold	implicate

Root	Meaning	Example
pneuma	wind, air	pneumonia
pon, pos, posit	put, place	dispose
port	carry	import
pseudo	false	pseudonym
psych	mind	psychology
press	press	compress
pyr	fire	pyromaniac
quir, quis	ask	inquire
rog	question	interrogate
scope	see	microscope
scrib, script	write	inscription
sect	cut	dissect
sequi	follow	sequence
sol	alone	solitude
soma	body	somatotype
somnia	sleep	insomnia
soph	wise	sophisticated
soror	sister	sorority
spect	look	inspect
spers	scatter	disperse
spir	breathe	inspire
struct	build	construction
tact	touch	tactile
tain, tent	hold	contain
tempo	time	temporary
the, theo	God	theology
therm	heat	thermometer
tort	twist	contort
tract	drag, pull	extract
verbum	word	verbatim
vis	see	revise

Prefixes

Prefix	Meaning	Example
a-, ab-	away, from	abduct
a-, an-	not, without	asexual
ac-, ad-	to, toward	accept, admit
ambi-, amphi-	both, around	ambivalent, amphitheater

Prefix	Meaning	Example
ante-	in front of, before	antecedent
anti-	against, oppose	antisocial
auto-	self	automatic
bi-	two, twice	bifocal
cata-, cath-	down, downward	catacombs
cent-	hundred	centennial
chrono-	time	chronological
circum-	around	circumspect
col-, com-, con-	with, together	collate, combine, connection
contra-	against	contradict
de-	down away, reversal	destruction
deca-	ten	decade
demi-	half	demigod
di-, duo-	two	dioxide
dia-	between, through	diagonal, dialogue
dis-	apart, away, in different directions	dismiss
dys-	ill, hard	dysfunctional
e-, ex-	out, from	emerge, expel
epi-	on, near, among	epidemic
eu-	good	euphoric
extra-	beyond, outside	extramarital
hecto-	hundred	hectogram
hemi-	half	hemisphere
hetero-	other, different	heterosexual
homo-	same	homonym
hyper-	above, excessive	hyperactive
hypo-	under	hypodermic
il-, im-, in-	not	illogical, impossible
im-, in-	in, into, on	implant, inject
infra-	lower	infrastructure
inter-	between, among	intercede
intra-	within	intranet
iso-	equal	isometric
juxta-	next to	juxtapose
mal-	wrong, ill	malpractice

Prefix	Meaning	Example
meta-	about	metaphysical
micro-	small	microscope
mil-	thousand	millennium
mis-	wrong	mistake
mono-	one	monotone
multi-	many	multimedia
non-	not	nonactive
nona-	nine	nonagon
octo-	eight	octopus
omni-	all	omniscient
pan-	all	panorama
penta-	five	pentagram
per-	through	pervade
peri-	around	periscope
poly-	many	polygon
post-	after, behind	postscript
pre-	before	precede
pro-	forward, on behalf of	promote
proto-	first	prototype
quadri-	four	quadrant
quint-	five	quintuplets
re-	back, again	retract
retro-	backward	retrospect
semi-	half	semicircle
sesqui-	one and a half	sesquicentennial
sex-	six	sextet
sub-, sup-	under, from below	subgroup, support
super-	above, over, beyond	supervise
sym-, syn-	together, with	symmetry, synonym
tele-	far, from a distance	telegraph
tetra-	four	tetrahedron
trans-	across	transport
tri-	three	triangle, triplet
ultra-	excessive, beyond	ultrasonic
un-	not	unnecessary
uni-	one	uniform
vice-	in place of	viceroy

Suffixes

Suffix	Meaning	Example
Noun suffixes	*People, places, thing*	
-acle, -acy, -ance	quality, state	privacy
-an	of, related to	American
-ant, -ary	one who, one that	servant
-arium, -ary	place or container	auditorium
-ation	action, process	education
-ator	one who	spectator
-cide	kill	homicide
-eer, -er, -ess	person, doer	collector
-ence, -ency	quality, state	residence, residency
-ent	one who, one that	president
-hood	quality, condition, state	brotherhood
-ician	specialist	statistician
-ism	belief	modernism
-ist	person	extremist
-ity	quality, trait	sincerity
-logy	study of	biology
-ment	act, state	statement
-ness	quality, condition, state	illness
-or	person, doer	juror
-path	practitioner; sufferer of a disorder	osteopath; psychopath
-ship	quality, condition, state	relationship
-tion	action, state	fraction
-tude	quality, degree	multitude
-y	quality, trait	apathy
Adjective suffixes	*Descriptions of nouns*	
-able	capable of	reusable
-ac, -al, -an, -ar, -ative	of, like, related to, being	logical
-ent	of, like, related to, being	persistent
-ful	full of	fearful
-ible	capable of	defensible
-ic, -ical, -ile, -ious, -ish, -ive	of, like, related to, being	feverish
-less	without	luckless

APPENDIX B

Foreign Words and Phrases

While many words in your dictionary have evolved from Greek and Latin word parts, some words have remained intact from their original form. These foreign words and phrases will appear in your everyday use as well as in some academic settings.

French

1. au courant (ō′ko͞o-räN′) adj. [in the current] informed; knowledgeable; up-to-date
2. bête noire (bĕt nwär′) n. [black beast] person or thing that is so disliked that one tries to avoid it
3. connoisseur (kŏn′ə-sûr′, -so͞or′) n. expert in fine arts or trained to have good taste

German

4. doppelgänger (dŏp′əl-găng′ər) n. ghostly double of a living person
5. zeitgeist (tsīt′gīst′) n. [spirit + time] spirit of the time; current trend

Latin

6. ad infinitum (ăd ĭn′fə-nī′təm) adj./adv. [to infinity] having no end
7. carpe diem (kär′pĕ dē′ĕm′) interj. [seize the day] seize the day; a caution to capture the pleasures of the moment and stop worrying about the future
8. mea culpa (mā′ə kŭl′pə) n [through my fault] an acknowledgment of error or fault

Spanish

9. aficionado (ə-fĭsh′ē-ə-nä′dō) n.[to induce a liking for] a follower; fan
10. tapas (tä′päs) n. pl. small, tasteful dishes served as a snack or served as a meal with others

APPENDIX C

Partial Answer Key

Chapter 1

Exercise 1A

1. b
2. c
3. d
4. a
5. a

Exercise 2A

1. c
2. b
3. a
4. d
5. a

Exercise 3A

1. c
2. a
3. b
4. a
5. c

Exercise 4A

1. d
2. c
3. a
4. b
5. c

Exercise 5A

1. b
2. c
3. a
4. c
5. d

Chapter 3

1. d
2. a
3. b
4. a
5. d
6. d
7. a
8. c
9. a
10. b

Chapter 4

1. a
2. b
3. c
4. b
5. d
6. c
7. a
8. b
9. b
10. d

Chapter 5

1. a
2. d
3. b
4. c
5. a
6. d
7. c
8. a
9. c
10. b

Chapter 6

1. a
2. c
3. b
4. d
5. a
6. c
7. a
8. d
9. d
10. b

Chapter 7

1. b
2. c
3. a
4. a
5. d
6. c
7. d
8. a
9. d
10. a

Chapter 8

1. b
2. c
3. a
4. d
5. d
6. d
7. b
8. a
9. d
10. c

Chapter 9

1. c
2. a
3. d
4. a
5. c
6. c
7. b
8. b
9. c
10. b

Chapter 10

1. b
2. a
3. d
4. d
5. b
6. a
7. c
8. d
9. a
10. a

Chapter 11

1. d
2. c
3. a
4. c
5. a
6. b
7. b
8. a
9. c
10. d

Chapter 12

1. c
2. b
3. b
4. c
5. a
6. a
7. d
8. b
9. b
10. d

Chapter 13

1. d
2. c
3. a
4. c
5. d
6. a
7. a
8. b
9. d
10. c

Chapter 14

1. d
2. a
3. a
4. d
5. c
6. b
7. b
8. a
9. b
10. b

Chapter 15

1. a
2. b
3. b
4. c
5. d
6. c
7. d
8. d
9. c
10. a

Chapter 16

1. b
2. a
3. b

4. d
5. c
6. a
7. a
8. a
9. c
10. a

Chapter 17

1. c
2. c
3. a
4. b
5. d
6. d
7. a
8. b
9. a
10. a

Chapter 18

1. d
2. c
3. c
4. a
5. d
6. b
7. d
8. a
9. a
10. d

Chapter 19

1. a
2. c
3. d
4. a
5. a
6. b
7. c
8. a
9. b
10. c

Chapter 20

1. d
2. c
3. a
4. b
5. a
6. b
7. c
8. a
9. a
10. c

Chapter 21

1. a
2. b
3. a
4. a
5. b
6. d
7. a
8. c
9. c
10. b

Chapter 22

1. a
2. b
3. d
4. d
5. c
6. d
7. a
8. b
9. b
10. a